Derps

To Whom Do We Belong?
An Ignatian Retreat

by David L. Fleming SJ

Review for Religious
St. Louis, Missouri
2009

Acknowledgment

I want to express my deep gratitude to William Hart McNichols, iconographer, for use of his icon "St. Ignatius Amidst Alaska." The icon captures well the theme of this book.

Cover with permission: "St. Ignatius Amidst Alaska"
©William Hart McNichols
St. Andrei Rublev Icons.com
<www.fatherbill.org>.

© 2009 Review for Religious
All rights reserved
Printed in the United States of America

Dedication

To all those who have been important
to my experience of belonging:

To my father and mother, both deceased,
to my sisters Marian and Jean—
the family to whom I belong;

to my Jesuit companions,
especially my 1952 entrance class
and my 1965 ordination class—
my vowed family with whom I have lived
the major part of my life;

to all those who have been part of the Ignatian family
that I have been privileged to know, love, and serve.

Contents

Foreword

In June 2009, I was invited to lead the annual eight-day retreat for the Jesuits of the Missouri and New Orleans provinces. I chose as the theme for this retreat the question "To whom do we belong?" The retreat format was simple: I would give one presentation a day, with suggestions for three or four prayer periods spread throughout the day. The retreat began with an opening conference in the evening and closed with a presentation, Mass, and a mid-day lunch.

In preparing these presentations for others than my Jesuit brothers, I have adapted what I said to my fellow Jesuits to embrace all those who find their spiritual lives enhanced by Ignatian spirituality. This retreat book does demand a familiarity with the *Spiritual Exercises* of St. Ignatius Loyola. The reader-retreatant ideally would have made the 30-day Exercises in its concentrated form within

30 days or through some months in everyday life. This person is conversant with the structural elements that Ignatius has created to help in the dynamic movement of the retreat. For example, when I speak of the Three Types of Persons or the Three Degrees of Humility, I expect that the retreatant has some knowledge and experience of these exercises from their previous retreat exposure. I recall and explain these various structural pieces in a way that is meant to enlighten the matter for prayer of that particular day and help in its assimilation.

To introduce the matter for prayer, I began each conference with a prayer focused on the grace that we seek for the day. I have included these prayers at the beginning of each day, and I have repeated them in the text at the end of the retreat-presentation outline and scripture references with which I conclude each presentation. I hope that these prayers might be used throughout the retreat day as a way of imbibing the grace of the day. Besides this book, then, it is necessary to have at hand a copy of the *Spiritual Exercises* of St. Ignatius and a Bible.

Let me thank my fellow Jesuits who first experienced these presentations in making their annual retreat. Their own prayer and support encouraged me in preparing this version of a retreat that might be helpful for others. I am also grateful to my staff at the journal Review for Religious who took on the extra work of producing this book. The staff includes Father Philip Fischer SJ, Mary Ann Foppe, Tracy Gramm, and Judy Sharp.

I pray that those who use this book for their retreat and prayer time will find their lives enriched and graced as they respond to the question "To whom do we belong?"

7

David L. Fleming SJ

Prayer for Entering the Retreat

Jesus, we are in your presence with one desire.

We ask and we want with all our heart

to have you close to us all the days of this retreat.

We will try to pray, we will stay focused,

we will spend our time with you.

But it is only with your grace and your love

that we, in our weakness, can remain faithful.

Jesus, be our companion and brother.

Amen.

Being Companions of Jesus

For members of the Society of Jesus, there is one essential friendship that gives direction to our life together: we all are companions of Jesus and so companions to one another. This is our Jesuit-focused vocational variation on the double commandment: love of God and love of neighbor. In fact, what allows us to be a religious order is the fact that we find ourselves called to be companions of Jesus first and so we find ourselves companions to one another—all because of our personal relationship with Jesus and with his mission. That vision has been given to us by Ignatius, especially in his Call of the King meditation from the *Spiritual Exercises*.

This vision is expanded to all those who find life in their responding to Ignatian spirituality. We find our vocation lived out as companions of Jesus. From the vision presented in the Call of the King meditation we know that we are always working with others, all of us called by the Risen Jesus to be with and to work with him.

The general theme for our retreat is expressed in the question: To whom do we belong? We often take

9

for granted our relationship with Jesus. After all, aren't we people who have been baptized in the name of Jesus? Don't we pray to him? Isn't all that we do in our family and community life and in our ministry—whether it be our mutual caring for one another, our volunteering, our parish involvement, our work environment, even our incidental conversations—all done in his name? Isn't just being a Catholic and doing what Catholics do enough to speak about our relationship with Jesus?

Like all relationships—marriage being a prime example in our own experience of our families and friends—either we are growing and deepening in our togetherness or we are letting the relationship grow cold and letting it deteriorate and die. Like all relationships that are alive and well, we need to work at our relationship with Jesus. It always needs to be growing, or else it is in some kind of dying process.

The primary focus of these retreat days will be reviewing, renewing, and deepening our relationship with Jesus. In looking at our relationship with Jesus, we are at the same time looking at our relationship with one another since Jesus himself has said that he is present where two or three are gathered.

Our prayer form will draw from the Ignatian way of contemplating the Gospel scenes as well as the various forms of Ignatian reviews called examens, particularly, the examen of prayer after each prayer period and the consciousness examen at the end of the day. Sometimes I will also suggest a meditative approach or a *lectio divina* way of praying.

For our prayer exercises for each day of the retreat, I will give some general comments about the prayer content and its application through points, but for those of you who may use this book and at the same time work with a director, I defer to the ways that your director finds that he or she can be most helpful to you in pointing the retreat. For example, I am suggesting that you might find four prayer periods each day a good pattern for your retreat: a prayer period in the morning upon arising, and then three periods spaced between morning, afternoon, and evening time. Some may find that three prayer periods better fit their energy and need for some relaxed time. Either you with your director or you with God figure out what appears to be better for you at this time. Remember Ignatius's basic dictum: it is not more periods of prayer but the savoring of our prayer that is important.

I will usually be suggesting three different scripture passages each day that you might use for your prayer time. As you know in the Exercises, Ignatius indicates no more than two passages of content for any one day of a retreat followed by repetitions and an application of the senses. But at the same time in the 30-day Exercises, Ignatius grants that an adaptation might be adopted in the Third and Fourth Weeks of the full Spiritual Exercises which would allow for new content in each prayer period. In this adapted retreat, if one were to be praying three contemplations a day, then there would be no Ignatian repetition. If one were to be praying four prayer periods a day, then the fourth period could be an Ignatian repetition. You remember that for an Ignatian repetition it is not a matter of returning to the scripture passage as such or some kind of blending of two or more texts but rather a review of one's noting in your prayers' examens where consolations and desolations occurred and returning to those moments as a way of "repeating." From Ignatius's insight, it is there in those moments that God will meet us—again.

I will be sharing with you my own understanding of various aspects of Ignatius's *Spiritual Exercises* throughout this retreat as a context for our prayer. I intend to use certain structures of the Exercises to help us to enter into

11

our theme of belonging to Christ. Hopefully whatever insight I might have into the Exercises will be given in such a way that it will enhance your own understanding and ability to enter into the retreat more full-heartedly. Similar to our relationship with Jesus, we as people who find our spiritual life enhanced by Ignatian spirituality should always be growing in our understanding of and in our ability to work with the Ignatian Exercises as an essential part of our Ignatian ministry. Our every retreat is a time not only for our own spiritual growth but also for our growing experience in this way of ministering. We pray, and we also learn.

Typical of an eight-day retreat, we will be adapting and accommodating the Exercises of Ignatius. I describe that the grace we seek during this retreat is better expressed in its Second Week form. What is it that we seek—the *id quod volo*? We pray for the grace that we might come to know Jesus more intimately, that we might love him more, and follow him more closely. That grace seems to sum up the focus of the direction of our retreat in being and growing as companions of Jesus. Of course, any one day of the retreat can have a more specifically focused grace that is being asked for.

I will introduce each conference with a prayer and repeat the prayer at its closure. Perhaps you will find these prayers focused on each day's content helpful in your own prayer periods or at times used within the day.

In this first conference, I am proposing that we begin where Ignatius ends in the prayer periods of the Exercises—with the Contemplation on the Love of God. Why might we begin where Ignatius ends? The most basic reason is that by beginning with the Contemplation on the Love of God we might more easily remember where we have left off from our last retreat. I will recall that there has been a way of understanding the Contemplation on the Love of God as summarizing in its four points the movement of all Four Weeks of the Exercises. For example, Michael Buckley SJ some thirty years ago laid out such an explanation in *The Way* journal. By our returning to this prayer exercise to begin our retreat, we might find ourselves recapturing that special Week's graces which were God's gift in our last retreat.

Sometimes we act as if every annual retreat we have made is a discrete movement, having little or no impact from our past life or on our present living. The Ignatian annual retreat needs to have its context of where God has met us in our last retreat and what fruit it has borne in the way we have been living our life up till the time of this present retreat, upon which we are now embarking. So we have the prayer time tonight and/or tomorrow morning for us to get in touch with the grace of our last retreat. It is from our gratitude for that grace that we launch into our prayer time now.

There is one major change that I am proposing for our approach to the *Contemplatio* as a help to focus the grace. I am placing Jesus or Christ wherever we find the word *God*. I want us to approach this first introductory prayer period as a way of beginning this retreat of looking at our relationship to Jesus. Whether we pray tonight or tomorrow morning or use this matter for both periods, I want us to find the points of the *Contemplatio* Christ-centered.

For a first prelude I suggest that we place ourselves before our favorite image of Christ. Or perhaps it is not an image but his presence in the Blessed Sacrament. For the grace we seek I propose that we ask simply that Jesus grace us with his loving presence during these days.

I suggest using the usual four points of Ignatius's contemplation. If we have the text of the Exercises, we will find them at *Sp Ex* [230] – [237]. No matter if we do not

13

have the text, since I will review the four points for all of us, with the emphasis on Jesus.

In the first point of the *Contemplatio*, Ignatius focused our attention on the creative act of God, his first redeeming act, in calling us to come to know God through the many gifts of our created world. We praise and reverence our God by the love-choices we make in our living in this Garden of God by our care and service of this world, thereby handing our world and ourselves back to the God from whom we came. For Ignatius, this sums up the Principle and Foundation with which the Exercises begins and the First Week material, especially viewed with our eyes on the eyes of Christ on the cross, in the first colloquy of the first exercise of the First Week.

If you prefer a scriptural approach with the focus on Christ, the scripture that likely inspired Ignatius is found in John's Gospel, chapter one, and in Paul's letter to the Colossians, chapter one. As John writes:

> In the beginning was the Word; the Word was in God's presence, and the Word was God. He was present to God in the beginning. Through him all things came into being, and apart from him nothing came to be. Whatever came to be in him, found life, life for the light of men. The light shines on in the darkness, a darkness that did not overcome it. . . .The real light which gives light to every man was coming into the world. He was in the world, and through him the world was made, yet the world did not know who he was. To his own he came, yet his own did not accept him. Any who did accept him he empowered to become children of God. . . . The Word became flesh and made his dwelling among us and we have seen his glory: the glory of an only Son coming from the Father, filled with enduring love (Jn 1:1-5, 9-12, 14).

Let me briefly reflect on the passage. Jesus, Son of God, the very expression of God, the Word of God, is the source

14

of all creation because all created things are "expressions of God." As Ignatius notes, all of creation is God's gift, intended to help us to know God and so to better respond to God, the Giver of gifts. Jesus in his very life and in his words sheds light upon the confusing and dark areas of our human world. Jesus gave to us a fullness of understanding of what God intends by creating us in the image of his only-begotten Son. Jesus, God's total gift of self to us, intends to make real for us that we are not just creatures created by a loving God but that God really wants to make us— the created ones—to be part of God's family, to be taken into God's triune life forever. By his human birth, God's Son—Jesus—made his dwelling (literally, "pitched his tent or tabernacle") among us—just as the Ark of the Covenant housed in a tent symbolized God's dwelling among the Israelites. Now Jesus' dwelling among us is not a symbol, but the reality. As a result, we can see God's glory—*glory*, meaning the visible manifestation of God, the shining out of God. Ignatius always wanted us to work in such a way that God was shining out through how we lived and what we did. Ignatius even called for us to give "greater" glory to God. *That's* a tall order for us at all times.

In St. Paul's letter to the Colossians, Paul writes:

> He [Jesus] is the image of the invisible God, the first-born of all creatures. In him everything in heaven and on earth was created, things visible and invisible, whether thrones or dominations, principalities or powers; all were created through him and for him. He is before all else that is. In him everything continues in being. It is he who is head of the body, the Church; he who is the beginning, the first-born of the dead, so that primacy may be his in everything. It pleased God to make absolute fullness reside in him and, by means of him, to reconcile everything in his person, both in earth and in the heaven, making peace through the blood of his cross (Col 1:15-20).

15

The lyricism of Paul in this passage presents a high Christology that still is rooted in our experience. From the Book of Genesis, we have always said that we are created in the image and likeness of God. But, with Jesus, we acknowledge that he is the actual likeness of God, and he has come into the world to offer us the reality of that likeness—a reality that raises us up beyond any angels or super-powers. By his resurrection, Jesus takes his place as the head of a new body—the Mystical Body—the Church. In some mysterious way, all things—in heaven and on earth—will find their unity in him. But reconciliation comes at a cost, the cost of the cross. What we drink in from the scripture passages from John and from Paul is that all of creation is Christ-centered and God's gifting us is centered in the gift of Jesus.

Let me more quickly review with you the other Ignatian points. For the second point, Ignatius suggests that we consider the way that God not only creates, but also shows his presence in his creation. In the Gospel of St. Matthew, Jesus is identified in the angel's announcement to Joseph as Emmanuel, God-is-with-us. And Jesus, in the last verse of St. Matthew's Gospel, repeats that "I will be with you always, until the end of the world." In his Eucharistic presence, Jesus is tangibly always with us.

In the Ignatian third point, we have an emphasis on a God who continues to labor in his creation. We remember well from the Call of the King meditation that Ignatius imaged Jesus calling us to be with him and *to labor* with him. All our Ignatian spirituality is based on, not *our* laboring, but on our trying to be helpful in working with Jesus in *his* labors for the Kingdom, even now. Jesus always has the lead, and we want to work with him. Do we need to clarify for ourselves that this is the vision and reality out of which we work?

To Whom Do We Belong?

In the fourth point, Ignatius focuses on the totalizing aspect of God's enveloping love—like the sunlight that envelops our earth, like the ever-continuing flow of water from a spring. What is our experience of this in our relation with Jesus? It is our confession of how totalizing is our response to Jesus through Thomas's words, "My Lord and my God." It is our way of saying: "Jesus, you are everything for me. You are my All." Ignatius responds: ". . . your love and your grace—*that* is enough for me."

We remember that Ignatius gives us his own prayer colloquy to say after each of these four points. It is our "Take and receive" prayer. He explicitly allows for its adaptation by the retreatant so that the colloquy can always remain our personal response to God—for us in this prayer period, specifically to Jesus.

Whatever the grace you recall from your last retreat, let yourself enjoy the consolation of this first prayer about the way that Christ shows his love for us.

17

Entering the Retreat

Being Companions of Jesus

Review Outline

- basic theme of our retreat: to whom do we belong?
- our one essential friendship as Catholics: our relationship with Jesus
- our approach: through Ignatian contemplations and Ignatian prayer examens and the daily consciousness examen
- the retreat grace we seek: to know Christ more intimately that we might love him more and follow him more closely
- Contemplation on the Love of God: a way of entering into retreat through a recapturing where our last retreat may have taken us
- the grace of this prayer period: that Jesus grace us with his presence in these days of retreat

Prayer Points

1) Jesus as Word in whom all things are created (e.g. John 1 and Colossians 1)
2) Jesus as Emmanuel, God-with-us
3) Jesus as the One who works like his Father
4) Jesus as "My Lord and my God," my All

Prayer

Jesus, we are in your presence with one desire.
We ask and we want with all our heart
to have you close to us all the days of this retreat.
We will try to pray, we will stay focused,
we will spend our time with you.
But it is only with your grace and your love
that we, in our weakness, can remain faithful.
Jesus, be our companion and brother.
Amen.

Prayer for the First Day

Jesus, you give yourself to us in every Eucharist.
All you ask is that we join our hearts to yours
in your ever-present gift of belonging to God.
Deepen in us our love for the Mass
as the center of our Catholic life.
Help us to live out its mystery in our lives of service.
Jesus, be the food and drink of our life.
Amen.

Our Foundation: The Last Supper

One of the struggles that St. Paul had with the Corinthian community was the division caused by allegiance to different teachers or preachers. Paul quotes individual members proudly saying "I belong to Paul" or "I belong to Apollo." But Paul responds, "Don't we all belong to Christ?"

It is a question that we do not often ask ourselves: to whom do we belong? Perhaps some of us do not even like the language. We might want to say that we are free and we don't *belong* to anyone. Others might say that "belonging" is a word without much meaning since they "belong" to all kinds of things: belong to this particular family, belong to this parish, belong to the neighborhood association or the AARP, belong to the CLC or the Ignatian Volunteer Corps, and so on. But Paul's question to the Corinthian community remains a central question for each one of us. To whom do we belong? It goes to the heart of our Ignatian vocation.

21

To whom do I belong is the question that Ignatius pictures Jesus definitively answering in the Third Week of the *Spiritual Exercises*. If I were to be asked, what is the centerpiece of the Spiritual Exercises, I would respond that the Third Week better fits that designation because of this answer of Jesus. Let me backtrack and say, first of all, I am not sure that talking about *a* centerpiece of the Exercises is meaningful. As I understand the Exercises, each Week has its own movement and its own focused relationship with God. I would suspect, however, that many, including most Jesuits, would identify the Second Week as central to the Exercises just because it is the most developed Week of the book, with the greatest number of Ignatian structures within it. Don't we discern a vocation call or a reform of life in the Second Week and aren't the Third and Fourth Weeks just a confirmation of what went on in the Second Week? *That* is the common perception that most of us have heard and read in various commentaries on the Exercises.

It is true that in the Second Week exercises we are searching out how God is calling us as we contemplate Jesus following his vocation call. And we may come through discernment during these Second Week contemplations to some sense of how we might follow out God's will for us in our life-direction. We are walking towards our answer to that question: to whom do we belong? And *that* question is the central question of the Exercises that we are trying to answer. As we follow Jesus into the Third Week, we find ourselves accompanying Jesus as he answers the question by giving himself over to God the Father by his death on the cross. Jesus is saying to us: from God have I come, to God do I go. I am giving myself back to God. "Into your hands I commend my spirit." By our being with Jesus and by following Jesus in this Third Week, we find ourselves in our own compassionate way accompanying

Jesus in our own way of surrendering ourselves to God as the One to whom we belong.

One of our great Jesuit theologians of the 20th century was Karl Rahner. A central point of his pastoral and spiritual theology is that we spend our lives learning how to die. What Rahner meant by that striking statement is that we are always learning how to give ourselves over, to surrender, to God. Death, the moment of death, is our special moment to exercise our freedom in making that ultimate gift of self to God. Surrender or giving ourselves over to another does not come easy for us. So we know how important it is for us to practice if we want to perform an action well. That is the reason why Rahner can say that we spend our lives *learning* how to die. Every action that we take which is a giving over of ourselves— life-changing as in the giving-over in marriage, as in the giving-over in religious vows, as in priestly ordination or reform-of-life changing as in vocational choices in serving the poor through the Catholic Worker community, in serving with the L'Arche community, in volunteering with the Red Cross disaster relief—is an important moment in our learning process of dying. The simple, everyday act of giving ourselves over to sleep is a kind of dying movement that allows for new life upon our awakening. We can't make ourselves sleep; we have to give ourselves over or surrender. In fact, every time we give ourselves over, when we are the ones not in control, in other words, the times when we find ourselves obeying—we are learning how to die. Perhaps that is why Ignatius puts such great emphasis on the vow of obedience for Jesuits. In order to follow Jesus more closely, we are always learning how to die.

Although the historical moment, the point in time, when Jesus gave himself literally over to God was the moment of his death on the cross, Ignatius enters us into that moment by the key of the Last Supper. In our retreat, I want to use this Last Supper contemplation as our principle and foundation as we explore the question, "To whom do we belong?" Within the 30-day retreat, Ignatius intends that the Last Supper contemplation is a foundation for all the contemplations on the Passion. For Ignatius and for us, then, the first contemplation of the Third Week of the Exercises provides us with the key to enter into and understand all the events of the Passion. The contemplation of the Last Supper acts as a kind of principle and foundation for all the events of the Third Week. Without the Last Supper as our principle and foundation for the Third Week we stand outside the Passion and see only the external events. For Ignatius, looking at injustice, looking at betrayal, looking at suffering, looking at death is never enough. We must be able to enter in, to know compassion. In the Third Week, we need to pray to Jesus for the grace that he will enter us into his passion. Ignatius proposes three extra points or focuses, all dealing with the interior of Jesus' response, during these Third Week contemplations just to make sure that we do not stay on the outside, looking in. Our following of Jesus has taken a dramatic turn in the Third Week over the Second Week. Do we really *belong* to Jesus? Can we follow him in his belonging journey in this Third Week?

In order for us to establish our principle and foundation for this retreat, I want to focus our prayer time on this first day on the events of the Last Supper as Ignatius points them in his Exercises. We want to look full-on at what for Jesus it means "to belong to anyone." From this foundation prayer day, this beginning and at the same time the end-point, we can let the contemplations of the other days of this retreat continue to spell out for us how Jesus leads us on in this belonging direction.

Ignatius presents the Last Supper contemplation through three points: 1) Jesus and the apostles celebrating

24

the Passover supper, 2) Jesus' washing of the feet of the disciples, and 3) Jesus' instituting the Eucharist as "the greatest mark of his love." All the events are saying something about belonging.

For us to enter into this first point, some familiarity with the Exodus event and the origins of the Passover meal in the Old Testament are necessary. On the eve of the Exodus event in Egypt (Ex 12), Moses passed on to the Israelite people the instructions he had received from God. Each family was to kill a lamb, sprinkle its blood on the lintel of their house, and roast the lamb for food, as they stood dressed and ready for the journey. The blood on the lintel of their houses saved the Israelites from the angel of death visited upon the Egyptians and all their firstborn among humans and animals. The angel of death would "pass over" the Israelites' marked houses. The roasted lamb gave them the strength for their journey into the desert. The Israelites were to celebrate this paschal meal *in memoriam* and were presented with a ritual way of conducting the meal and remembering how God has been their savior and redeemer. By God's action, they were being set aside as a people special to God. In the same book of Exodus (Ex 24), we find the ritual of the covenant between God and his people. The ritual of the covenant is sealed by blood—blood is described as the "seat of life"—and the blood is sprinkled on the altar symbolizing God and on the people. By this sprinkling, God and the Israelite people were sharing the same "blood"; this was the covenant action that made this people "peculiarly" God's own. They belonged to God.

Jesus and his apostles were involved in this special Jewish meal of the Pasch or Passover, the celebration of God choosing and making a people his own. And it was Jesus, the Lamb of God, as the leader or *paterfamilias*, who recalled the events of the Exodus Passover as they

25

celebrated together. We have here the elements of a lamb, blood which is saving, food which is strengthening for the journey, and eventually the covenant notion, with God as redeemer. *Redeemer* is a word meaning for the Israelites a "blood-relative," and one who comes to the aid of a "family" member in every need. As Jesus says, "This cup is the new covenant in my blood" (Lk 22:20). Somehow the density or richness of this first Ignatian point dealing with the lamb as food for the journey and a new covenant in a redeeming blood is caught up in these elements. It could fill up a whole prayer period.

The second point is Jesus' washing of his apostles' feet. This account is the gospel of our Holy Thursday liturgy. Although Jesus asks the question "Do you understand what I just did for you?" he knows that the apostles cannot give an answer. Even for us today the density and richness of this Ignatian point will never be exhausted. Jesus' service action flows from his basic stance before God his Father and before us, his brothers and sisters. Jesus is, above all, the One who serves. As Ignatius tells us in his prenote to the Contemplation on the Love of God (*Sp Ex* [230 ff]), love is shown more in deeds than in words. And, Ignatius goes on to say, love is shown by a sharing between lovers, a sharing that speaks or communicates love. In this incident of washing the feet of his apostles, Jesus calls us "blest" if we put into practice, that is, "share," what we have learned. As the Church has indicated in its Holy Thursday liturgy, the Eucharist and the washing of the feet will always be intimately connected as the action of love, a belonging action. This point too can fill a whole prayer period.

Finally, the Ignatian third point is focused on Jesus' giving us his Body and his Blood in the form of bread and wine. What stands out in the text is Ignatius's identifying this action as "the greatest mark of his love," not, as we might expect, his death on the cross.

26

For Ignatius (and for us), the fulfillment of the paschal meal is *now* in this action of Jesus. In his love for God his Father and in his love for us, Jesus literally hands himself over to us to be our food for our life's journey. His blood allows for the new covenant between God and us, and with our drinking the communion cup we literally flow with divine blood. We are brothers and sisters with Jesus, and brothers and sisters to one another, and children of God. The Eucharist is "the greatest mark of his [Jesus'] love" because this is the eternal stance of a love shared by Jesus with the Father and with us. In every Eucharist, we enter into the timeless or, better said, the NOW moment of Jesus' love—a love so complete that nothing is held back in its sharing. The love of Jesus, expressed in this first Eucharist, remains a total giving over or surrender as we see it played out in all the events of the passion and death of Jesus. In his Eucharistic sharing Jesus continues to bear all costs, so that even today our attempts to kill, to ignore, to run away, and to deny cannot stifle this love. In his loving action we might see Jesus belonging to us; in reality it is in every communion that we live out the action of belonging to him.

This contemplation on the Last Supper is like the foundation of all the other contemplations on the Passion. If we do not build on this foundation of the Third Week we too easily get caught up in only how awful is Jesus' suffering, how many stripes he bore, how long he hung on the cross. Yes, the costs for Jesus were terrible, but we must never lose sight of the love that has him enter into the cost, whatever it is. The passion and crucifixion of Jesus are time bound; these events happened once. Jesus' love captured in the Eucharist is the NOW event that each one of us can touch and enter into. It is through the Eucharist that we can come to know compassion with Christ. He still bears the costs of love, but *through us* as we in our faith deal with one another and with our world.

I believe that it is from his mystical experience that Ignatius had the insight into the Eucharist as "the greatest mark of his love." You may remember that Ignatius relates in his *Autobiography* that he had five mystical experiences at Manresa. One of these dealt with how Jesus is present in the Eucharist. I do not think that Ignatius was seeing some kind of physical body or image of Jesus in the host. As the priest held up the host at the time of the consecration, Ignatius saw white rays coming down from heaven. At that moment, Ignatius understood the eternal stance of Jesus offering himself to the Father in the gesture of the priest, and the eternal stance of Jesus offering himself to us in the rays coming down from heaven. *That* is how Jesus is present in the Eucharist. The Eucharist, then, for Ignatius remains the key for us to enter into what it means for Jesus to belong to God.

The Eucharist speaks of the eternally active sharing of Jesus' love for his Father and for us celebrated in every Mass—Ignatius's mystical vision. The Mass will always be at once a meal and a sacrifice—Jesus' surrendering love to us to be our food for the journey and Jesus' surrendering love to his Father to be one with him forever. An unjust and cruel death becomes the costly means for Jesus to surrender himself in love to his Father, a sacrificial love, a love that makes holy—a return journey to belong to God from whom he had come. In his love surrender to us, even as we humans take his life, Jesus shows us the way for us to journey, along with him, in order to finally belong to God, the One we too call "Our Father."

Let us take a step back for a moment. Remember that throughout the Second Week of the Exercises we pray that we might be graced with an intimacy with Jesus so that we might *follow* him more closely. In the Second

28

Week our focus is on Jesus, particularly in all the activities of his public life. As we move into the Third Week, Ignatius continues to emphasize our *following* of Jesus. In the Third Week our following of Jesus is no longer in his active ministry, but now in what is happening to him, what is being imposed on him. Our intimacy and following of Jesus must take in the whole of life, both the whole of Jesus' life (what he does and what happens to him) and the whole of our lives (what we do and what happens to us). Ignatius subtly lets us experience a whole new level of intimacy (and discipleship) with Jesus as we enter into the contemplations of the Third Week, with the Eucharist as our foundation contemplation. Eucharist is about Jesus taking the whole of his life and surrendering it to God and to us. Eucharist (the Mass) for us is our attempt to take the whole of our life—Sunday by Sunday, or day by day—and to surrender it to God and to our fellow human beings. As Jesus lives, so we live. We live out of our "belonging" with Jesus in the gift of ourselves with him to the Father in every Eucharist. Our belonging to Christ receives its foundation in our contemplating the meaning of the Last Supper.

For your prayer periods, I suggest that you might take one of Ignatius's points for the Last Supper: 1) Exodus 12 and 24 for the paschal meal and covenant ritual; 2) the washing of the feet in John 13; and 3) Jesus' giving the Eucharist in Matthew 26. Another possibility is to reflect on the giving of the Eucharist in each of the Synoptic Gospels: 1) Matthew 26:26-30; 2) Mark 14:22-26; and 3) Luke 22:14-20. The grace we seek today: the grace to experience our belonging to Jesus as we celebrate the Eucharist.

29

First Day

Our Foundation: The Last Supper

<u>Review Outline</u>

- A life question: to whom do we belong?
- Jesus' answer is definitively expressed in the Third Week
- Karl Rahner: we spend our lives learning how to die
- Ignatian insight: Last Supper is key to all the Third Week contemplations
- Jesus in the Eucharist acts out to whom he belongs and invites us in every Eucharist to join with him
- The grace we pray for: Jesus, grace us with our belonging to you in our Eucharist today

<u>Prayer Points:</u> 2 approaches to choose

a. Use the Ignatian three points, one for each prayer period
   1) Jesus' celebrating the paschal meal and covenant ritual: Exodus 12 and Exodus 24
   2) Jesus' washing of the feet: Jn 13
   3) Jesus' giving of the Eucharist: Mt 26:26-30

b. Use the Synoptic Gospel accounts of the Last Supper
   1) Matthew 26:26-30
   2) Mark 14:22-26
   3) Luke 22:14-20

Prayer

Jesus, you give yourself to us in every Eucharist.

All you ask is that we join our hearts to yours

in your ever-present gift of belonging to God.

Deepen in us our love for the Mass

as the center of our Catholic life.

Help us to live out its mystery in our lives of service.

Jesus, be the food and drink of our life.

Amen.

Prayer for the Second Day

Jesus, we know you
as the One who has called us
to our special following of you.
Help us now to keep listening to your calls
as you lead us in our faith journey.
Stir up in us a readiness to be with you
in whatever task you do.
Jesus, be our leader and guide.
Amen.

Second Day

Jesus' Initiative:
The Call of the King

A rich, structural exercise that Ignatius wrote to begin the Second Week of the *Spiritual Exercises* is titled The Call of the King. We commonly refer to it as the Kingdom meditation. Referring to it as the Kingdom meditation makes it sound as if the prayer period is about the objective reality of the Kingdom of God. For Ignatius, the focus of the meditation is strictly personal; the focus is on the person of Jesus. The grace that Ignatius suggests that we pray for is "not to be deaf to his call but to be ready and diligent" to make our response. The exercise is all about our relationship with Jesus—our belonging to Jesus—and our acting on this relationship.

Ignatius, good theologian that he was and correct observer of Scripture, sees that the initiative of God's saving action is always with God. Both in the Old Testament and in the New, God is the One who is first to call into our lives. In the Old Testament, we see God's taking the

33

initiative in his call to Abraham, in God's call to Moses, in God's call to David, in God's call to Isaiah and Jeremiah and to each of the prophets. When we consider the Gospels in the New Testament, what impresses us in each of the Gospels is the call that Jesus makes to his apostles. In the synoptic Gospels, Jesus simply says, "Follow me." And the immediacy of the following by Peter and Andrew and James and John and the tax collector Levi or Matthew is breathtaking. We do have an exception in Luke's account when Peter seems to back off and say "I am not worthy because I am a sinful man." Jesus ignores his protestation and just says in a poetic way "I am going to take you from being a fisher man to being a fisher of men." And Peter is pictured as immediately responding to Jesus' initiative.

When we want to look at the question "To whom do we belong?" we need to ask ourselves a prior question: "Where does it begin?" While Ignatius in the Call of the King exercise is stressing how Jesus takes the initiative in calling each one of us to be his follower, we may be more theologically correct in saying that God the Father is always the One who takes the initiative. For example, in the Transfiguration scene in the Gospel, it is the voice of the Father who says "This is my Beloved Son. *Listen* to him." God is taking the initiative, but points out that we are to listen to Jesus and his invitations and instructions. And Jesus consistently in the Gospel of John says that he speaks or does nothing but what the Father wants. We understand that neither Jesus' words nor his actions are anything but what the Father would say or would do. Jesus identifies himself with the Father's initiatives. In responding, then, to the call to follow Jesus, we are choosing to move in the direction of belonging to Jesus and, as we say at the end of the Canon in every Mass, "through him, with him, and in him," we belong to God the Father.

34

Jesus' call has two aspects—both of them essential for answering our question "To whom do we belong?" First, Jesus' call is the invitation to be with him. Ignatius uses the Spanish word *comigo*, "with me." Second is Jesus' call that if we are "with him," then we will also labor or work with him. Ignatius emphasizes throughout his text the word *with*—always every action is in union with Jesus. We do what we do because we belong to him.

In our citing of this Call of the King exercise, especially as we refer to it as the Kingdom meditation, we often fixate on the work. Of course, it is the work *we* do—surely for God and in God's name. But the work in our way of thinking and in our emotional involvement becomes *our* work. Its measure of success or failure solely rests upon our own effort. We may even hide behind some fuzzy thinking and language that would seem to make our work more religiously balanced. The reality, however, in the toll that our work takes upon our energy, our body, our emotions, our psyche, and our family and community life betrays our feeble defense. Whether we are at home, at the office or factory, or in active ministry, we know what it means to be caught up in our own little work-world. Ignatius, too, knew that this temptation would be with us all our lives. That is why the Call of the King will remain a constant challenge in the life of any follower of Jesus—from our young years to one hundred plus or whenever we die. Do we just work or are we with Jesus in *his* work?

Jesus asks us, "Are you with me?" What does it mean for us to be *comigo*—to be "with Jesus"? The grace that we will be praying for throughout the Second Week of the Exercises gives us Ignatius's understanding of what we mean and how we might grow in being companions with Jesus. Ignatius has us pray for the grace to know him intimately that we might love him more and so follow him more closely. It is obvious that Ignatius is moving us to the *magis* in our relationship with Jesus. We cannot be content with reading books about Jesus, seeing movies about Jesus, studying Christology, or even saying prayers to Jesus. Ignatius first tells us that to be with Jesus requires that we are growing by grace in a knowledge of Jesus that is "from within," "inside," an "interior knowledge." I prefer to use the expression "an intimate knowledge."

For us to know someone intimately means that we move from knowing "things" about someone to knowing someone from what we might call a "heart-knowledge." When two people marry, they are pledging to each other that they want to grow in this kind of heart-knowledge of each other throughout the rest of their lives together. We sometimes use the language of a "oneness of soul." By our vows we Jesuits in a similar way promise ourselves to a lifelong quest of coming to know Jesus intimately. When Christian married people are faithful to this lifelong growing intimate knowledge of each other, each aids the other at the same time to know what the intimacy with Jesus means for them as a couple and as individuals and how each might help the other to grow in this intimacy. Those following a celibate vocation or living a single life do not have this kind of special help to know Jesus that comes from the marriage intimacy experience. We as celibates may be blessed with the intimacy of a *celibate* friendship that mirrors this kind of marital help, and we may be graced even with a number of these friendships in the course of our Jesuit lives—in my own life, it has been both friendships with fellow Jesuits and friendships with other religious and lay, both men and women. We as Jesuits are also meant to experience in a different way—through the *extensions* of our friendships especially in ministry moments that are profoundly personal, such as those special revelatory moments in confession or retreat

36

or spiritual direction ministry when we are gifted with the meaning and experience of an intimacy more profound than even the other spouse or closest friend has received. That has been my blessed experience. It is a revelatory moment for us celibates to experience what it looks and feels like when we speak of our intimate relationship with Jesus. We as celibates or ones living the single life are meant to use these friendship moments as helps to our growing intimacy with Jesus. They are God's special gifts to us to help us in our knowledge and love and service of God, in and with Jesus.

When Ignatius pictures Jesus calling to each man, woman, and child, we need to keep reminding ourselves of two aspects of this call. The first is that the initiative keeps coming from Jesus; it is not a one-time call, and after our own first response, we are now on our own to pursue the relationship or not. Sometimes because of the dryness of our prayer or our lack of consistency in personal prayer, we begin to think of ourselves as the initiators, of ourselves trying to get Jesus' attention or of ourselves as trying to woo Jesus. Of course, what usually is going on at these times is that we are so self-focused on our effort and how we feel that we are not very capable of entering into any relationship. In an image with which we are familiar, Jesus still stands at the door knocking, while inside our house we are too busy with our own concerns and our own housekeeping that we do not even hear the knock. For Ignatius it is always a grace to be prayed for—that we not be deaf to his call. It is easy for us to say: the initiative is from Jesus. But we find it hard not to play God, to take matters in our own hands, to want things on our terms, to expect that our timing is God's timing.

The second aspect is the word *call*. I have struggled to find an English word that might better connote what the

37

call

biblical sense of *call* is. *Call* is not imaged in a hotel bell-hop screaming out "Call for Philip Morris." (I am using an old image from radio days that has memories mostly for those of us we identify as the older or more mature readers/retreatants.) *Call* is not like saying we made a telephone call. Calls from God are imaged well in the incident with young Samuel. God calls, and Samuel comes out of a sleep and runs to Eli, his mentor, his spiritual director, asking "Did you call me?" It is only on the third attempt that Eli realizes that the call is from God and so he instructs Samuel just to say "Here I am." Note that the call from God is insistent. God keeps calling. Because God is Love, the call is not a neutral "Hi, how are you?" The call is imbued with all the feeling and emotion of God's love. Because the call is love-initiated, God is powerless and waits for a human response. Love is always free; it cannot be commanded. What we understand when we speak of the commandment of love is the service that necessarily follows upon love. What Ignatius identifies as the "sharing" that lovers do can be viewed as the commandment or the exercise of true love. Love is always more than words or feeling as Ignatius identifies in his prenote on love; love demands the creative action that we find in our Trinitarian God. Although it is true that love cannot be commanded, we might be able to say that service can be commanded. We can at least say that the closer we come to loving like God, as Ignatius saw, the more graced we are to love and to serve in all things, *en todo amar y servir*.

Love – free

Love + service

When we hear the word *call*, then, we must remember that God's way of calling, Jesus' way of calling, is a call prompted by love. It is a call involving the desires of God. The call has an insistence about it. It is an initiative that has God's personal involvement. We can only pray that we can grow to be so totally involved in our response that we will live out our vocational call.

38

Something else we might learn from the example of God's call to Samuel. We need to notice Samuel's way of responding. "Here I am" is the basic response to God's call. "Here I am" stands for "ready and willing." If we are ready at the call of Christ, we are beginning to take the stance of belonging to him. We are willing and we want to be with him in his labors for the Kingdom. Jesus, like God his Father, is the One who works, and we are the ones privileged to work with him. No matter our Ignatian activity, the reality is that Jesus is the One who is working and I am Jesus' helper, working alongside. My working alongside Jesus—not Jesus working alongside me—is the correctly imaged stance of one who belongs to Christ.

Listening to the call of Christ is the stance identified in a special way for Jesuits as Jesuit obedience. As we know, the word *obedience* comes from the Latin *ob-audire* which means "to listen," "to listen carefully." Jesus identifies his life and his mission as an obedience to his Father. If we truly belong to Jesus, Ignatius knew that one virtue would signalize our life, but especially Jesuit life—the virtue of obedience. A phrase that comes readily—should we say "spontaneously"?—to one who serves obediently is "Here I am." Often we finish it with our Ignatian response to God expressed as "Send me."

An important element in the Ignatian exercise of The Call of the King within the context of the full 30-day Exercises is the fact that it does not suggest a colloquy, that is, a personal prayer response on our part. Instead, we are asked to listen to the response of persons who are zealous and on fire in their following of Jesus. I believe that this caution should remain with us in our prayer today. We should be sober in assessing ourselves as we question "To whom do we belong?" Yes, we are considering the Ignatian beginnings of looking at this question. We begin with the Call of the King exercise. No matter if

39

we are young and have our initial first fervor or if we are older and have the experience of betrayal and forgiveness and recommitment, it is good for us to take careful stock of the matter at hand. Let's look at the calls of Christ.

Our problem with using the Gospel call passages is that it seems to focus on the first call of Jesus as if it were the only one. Yet even in scripture, we see many calls. For example, we see the calls to Peter reflected in Jesus' response to "you are the Messiah," and "how many times must we forgive—seven times?" and "I will never leave you." In a similar way, we see the calls of Jesus to James and John not only in their first call to leave their boats and nets, but also in Jesus' further call to their wanting to call down fire on the Samaritans and to their desire to sit at the right and left hand of Jesus. We know that Jesus keeps calling and we need to look at those calls in our lives. We might consider now just the calls of Jesus in this past year or since our last retreat.

Let us consider more carefully who it is who is calling. What are the qualities of this call? Before we so readily move to the work we do, what is our relationship with Jesus with whom we always work? Perhaps it would be good for us to consider carefully, as Ignatius has expressed it, the response of magnanimous persons—persons zealous and on fire *Sp Ex* [97]-[98]. Does it awaken in us a great desire to be truly like them?

In order to find ourselves in Ignatian contemplation, I would like to suggest for a first prayer period the calling of the first followers we find in Matthew 4:18-22, with its emphasis on immediacy, or Luke 5:1-11, with its picture of Peter's hesitancy. It focuses on the first direct call of Jesus. For a second prayer period, I am suggesting a slightly different approach to Jesus' call as we see it portrayed in John 1:35-51. Again note how Jesus takes the initiative with his question to the two disciples fol-

40

lowing after him, "What are you looking for?" That is followed by Andrew's initiative in seeking out his brother Peter and then Jesus' initiative again in welcoming Peter. I believe that we might consider the call of other persons in our lives that has helped us to hear and know the call of Christ. If you were to use a third scripture passage, I am suggesting that we might consider the call to the Samaritan woman that we find in John 4:4-42. With the Samaritan woman, we have a more subtle dialogue through which Jesus calls this woman to be a follower. Note Jesus' initiative in asking for a drink of water to begin the conversation. The woman, like many of us, seems to throw up distracting question to Jesus, but Jesus keeps the focus on her call. Perhaps, like the Samaritan woman, we need to look at our mistakes, our sins, which have been the occasion for us to hear the call of Christ in our life again. She will be the one to take the initiative in introducing her fellow townspeople to Jesus by giving witness to her own faults and failings.

The grace that we are praying for is that we will be gifted with hearing the calls of Christ and responding anew with all our heart.

41

Second Day

Being Companions of Jesus

Review Outline

- the Call of the King emphasizes first our relationship with Jesus and then our work
- initiative is always with Christ: for us to be with and to work with him
- our lifelong effort is to know Jesus intimately, to belong to him
- God's (Jesus') call is insistent and love-motivated
- our response to God's call is "ready and willing" —availability
- Christian obedience is rooted in this response to the Call of Christ

Prayer Points

1) Matthew 4:18-22 and/or Luke 5:1-11
2) John 1:35-51
3) John 4:4-42

Prayer

Jesus, we know you
as the One who has called us
to our special following of you.
Help us now to keep listening to your calls
as you lead us in our faith journey.
Stir up in us a readiness to be with you
in whatever task you do.
Jesus, be our leader and guide.
Amen.

Prayer for the Third Day

Jesus, you remain always faithful to us.

We confess that we fail to be so true

in our following of you.

We find ourselves led by what we like.

We know our attachments make us less free.

Strengthen us, we pray, in our every decision

to choose to follow you ever more closely.

Jesus, be our power and our light.

Amen.

The Ignatian Three Classes: Choosing to Respond

There is an Ignatian structural exercise in the *Spiritual Exercises* which seems to be quite pedestrian and would seem to have little place outside of the full 30-day retreat. Traditionally it has been called The Three Classes of Men or, as I might render it, Three Types of Persons *Sp Ex* [149]-[155]. A more literal translation of Ignatius's Spanish is the Three Pairs of Men. It is not an inspiring or engaging exercise such as The Call of the King or The Two Standards. As a result, it does not readily find itself a part of any Ignatian adapted retreat.

Many generations of Jesuits up to Vatican II would have been quite familiar with the kind of exercise that we find in the Three Types of Persons. The kind of exercise it is becomes clear in Ignatius's use of the word *pairs*. There was a medieval tradition in moral education of using as examples a man and a woman, often given the names Titius and Bertha, to set up an example of a moral question or dilemma. By using a man and a woman,

45

it gave the breadth of an everyman and everywoman to every moral case. So what Ignatius has done in this exercise is to set up a choice or decision-making formed after the manner of a *casus conscientiae*. A *casus conscientiae* is what we refer to as a "case study." *Casus conscientiae*, literally a "conscience case," was a common way to continue an inservice training for priests in their handling confession problems. Men studying theology for priesthood would also exercise their pastoral acumen by working with conscience cases in their moral theology classes. In the Jesuit tradition, about once a month Jesuit communities would come together in their required recreation period after dinner (this was an exercise for only the priests in their own recreation room as we had separate recreation rooms for the priests, scholastics, and brothers in the pre-Vatican II days) to discuss a conscience case. It was meant to be a continuing education model and a way for us Jesuit priests to maintain our reputation for being good confessors. As in many ritualized rigidities in the Church before Vatican II, the *casus conscientiae* often lost its educational and practical applicability by focusing on esoteric and bizarre minutiae found in unusual cases. Because of its formalized rigidity, the loss of this practice from the Jesuit tradition in community life was not mourned after Vatican II. Admittedly, I never experienced this practice since it was already gone from apostolic community life when I returned to an ordinary community after my own ordination to the priesthood and my special studies.

For Ignatius, the Three Types of Persons was a meditative way of more generally considering how people come to make decisions. For example, in looking at the question in this retreat—to whom do we belong? What does it mean for us to belong to Jesus?—we know that we have different ways at coming to make a response to the question. But before we begin once again to try to make our response to the question, Ignatius would have us consider in an objective manner three common ways that people tend to come to make an answer to a question affecting their life.

What Ignatius uses as his problem example is the accomplished fact of people having acquired a certain amount of money in a less than ethical way and yet they like having it. To be honest, we are not very free when we like or are enamored with what we have. Our *affect*, as Ignatius would call it, is involved, and so we may find it hard to keep a balance. Now our problem is how do we come to a practical decision about handling this money in a Christlike way, a way that lets us arrive at our decision with a freedom from our affect, from our emotional or calculating involvement. Ignatius would have us consider three different ways that people approach this question.

The first group remains aware of the problem, but keeps putting off the decision because of their love attachment. Their attitude is that tomorrow is another day and perhaps we will have time and energy and a new-found freedom to take up the question and come to a resolution. Maybe someday, they tell themselves, they will not find themselves so tightly involved with this money question and the decision will come easy. But as Ignatius points out, this group finds all the tomorrows have happened and they die with never having resolved the question. We call them procrastinators.

A second group of people acknowledge the question, keep the discussion on the table, and even take some actions in other areas towards living their lives in a more Christlike way. These people make some effort to take action in good and righteous ways about many areas of their life. The question about the acquired money is the only area of their life that never gets resolved because of their affective involvement with it and their unfreedom

47

about even wanting to make a decision. These are the "all except this" people. "We got everything done, but the question of the money. . . ."

A third group is recognized by Ignatius for its willingness and readiness to face the question about the acquired money. They know that they like the money they have, and they experience their reluctance to face the issue. Yet they want to work at freeing themselves of their affect for this money. In taking up the question of what to do about the money acquired in some overly materialist way, they want to hold themselves free of their disordered liking as they make their decision. For Ignatius, the actual decision is not an integral part of the case study. The importance in the Ignatian case study is the degree of freedom with which we can come to any one particular decision when our attachments and our affect are acknowledged.

Ignatius is a realistic, down-to-earth man. He does not image us growing into some idealized human freedom that allows us to make every decision like an angel. Rather he sees us rising to the occasion of each particular major decision with a determined effort to free ourselves of the loves and likings that upset the balance in our decision-making abilities. The disordered love or affect is what makes Ignatian discernment so hard for us. We must make the effort to test our affect if we want to be free in making a Christlike decision.

Why are we considering the Three Types of Persons exercise at this point in our retreat? In our first day we took up what is our principle and foundation for this retreat—the Last Supper contemplation which begins the Third Week. This provides us with our context as we look at the question that St. Paul raises, "To whom do we belong?" Since we may too readily presume that we have already given our response however long we have lived Jesuit life or however long we have lived an Ignatian spiri-

48

tuality, we need to look at the answer that Jesus provides by his own life example. In our following of Jesus, we need to let him lead us to what belonging means for him and where it leads us. Our prayer contemplation on the Last Supper gives us Jesus' own summary of what belonging means and where it leads. From this foundation, we moved on in our second day to the question of where this belonging begins. Who starts it and what might it include? We re-examined the Ignatian Call of the King. We acknowledged, with Ignatius, that it might be better for us to look at the response of generous followers rather than trying to make our own protest of total dedication at this early part of the retreat. Today we take the time to examine ourselves about the probability of our less-than-adequate ways of following Jesus in our day-to-day Ignatian lives. Maybe we have promised too readily that we belong to Jesus, when we really have many areas of our lives where that may not be the reality.

As Ignatius would have us look at it in this Three Types of Persons exercise, where do we find ourselves in our decision about belonging to Christ when it comes to the particular decisions that affect our spiritual life? What other loves or likings take a certain precedence that really affects our total surrender to following Jesus? Do we really keep putting off a decision about a closer relationship with Jesus that would affect the time we take to pray, our participation in Mass, or the way we work with others? How do we evade making the decisions that would help us in a more intimate following of Jesus?

For our contemplations, I am going to suggest three examples of followers of Jesus making decisions about their ways of following Jesus more closely. I believe that these three examples might touch into areas of our lives that hinder us from our belonging to Jesus. They also might stimulate us to pick up on some of what we might

49

call our metaphorical "acquired goods" or "possessions that are not true to who we are or profess to be," that stand in the way of our full-hearted commitment to our belonging to Jesus.

The first example that we have is given by Peter. The occasion is when Jesus asks the question "Who do people say that I am?" and then its follow-up question, "Who do *you* say that I am?" Is there a typically embarrassed silence among these twelve men before Peter finally speaks up and proclaims, "You are the Messiah, the Son of the living God"? Jesus immediately praises Peter for the way that the Father has blessed him through such a gifting of the Spirit. Because of God's initiative with Peter, Jesus identifies this man as the foundation rock of the new community called church. Then Jesus proceeds to speak about the journey of his own life—from rejection by Jewish authority to suffering and death and being raised on the third day.

We are told that Peter takes Jesus aside. Peter may be feeling pretty confident that he has a direct line to the Spirit, and so what Peter thinks, the Spirit must think. Imagining such a journey possibility for himself as Jesus describes, Peter can say with much feeling, "God forbid that any such thing ever happen to you." Jesus is described as turning on Peter and saying, "Get out of my sight, you Satan!" Peter is no longer the rock of support and stability, but now Peter is the tempter: "You are trying to make me trip and fall. You are not judging by God's standards but by man's."

Peter, like us, can truly be led by the Spirit in his following of Jesus, but when it comes to suffering and hardship Peter is fast back to his human way of thinking. That's where he belongs. Where do we fall down in our closer following of Jesus? Does it happen when we have to make choices and decisions that involve hard things?

In a paradoxical way, it is not the question of the Ignatian example of money acquired unjustly and how to right the situation, but rather what is the cost that we have to pay in staying true to Jesus as our leader? When is the decision put off by us in our following Jesus more closely? Is it when the choice seems to be hard and involves a cost for us? Peter understands that we keep getting faced with decisions about a more intimate following of Jesus, and he can share his experience with us.

The second example is given by James and John. Jesus and his apostles were journeying to Jerusalem and wanted to pass through a Samaritan town where likely they were seeking to stay overnight. But the Samaritans would not welcome Jesus and friends because they were on their way to Jerusalem. James and John, good followers of Jesus that they were, the two who had asked him for seats at his right and left when he would come into his kingdom, immediately were incensed at this behavior of the Samaritans. They asked Jesus, "Lord, would you not have us call down fire from heaven to destroy them?" The scripture says in a quiet manner: Jesus turned toward them only to reprimand them.

What do James and John and we have in common in our following of Jesus? Sometimes in our following of Jesus, what we really like is the action of "wiping out the enemy." Any differing opinions or any new behaviors or ways of acting are categorized as "the enemy" and they must be destroyed. Following Jesus may be easy if there is only one way of following—and it is the way that *we* do it. We, like James and John, want to keep it simple: people are either with us or against us. Don't confuse us with shades of gray. Don't ask us to work with "others," meaning people who look different from us, have different languages and cultures, and maybe even different faiths. Is this all included in our belonging to Jesus? Are these

51

the very steps that lead us to a more intimate following of Jesus? James and John have some experience that they may share with us since they saw the look on Jesus' face as he turned toward them.

A third example we find through a more general grouping of the followers of Jesus. Jesus has been instructing his followers that he will give them his body to eat and his blood to drink and they will have life because of him. Jesus was aware that his disciples were murmuring in protest at what he had said. Eating his body, drinking his blood—how bizarre and how disgusting! He bluntly asks them, "Does it shake your faith?" Then he goes on to say that "no one can come to me unless it is granted him by the Father." The immediate response was that many of his disciples broke away and would not remain in his company. I believe that it is at this point that we have the saddest question Jesus asks in the Gospels: "Do you want to leave me too?" Peter again comes through for us if we are in any way hesitant to make an answer. "Lord, to whom shall we go? You have the words of eternal life. We have come to believe; we are convinced that you are God's holy one."

What do the apostles as a group have to share with us contemporary followers of Jesus? There will be times of confusion, discouragement, and even defeat. Where does our love, our affect go at such times? Does it get expressed like this, not letting us be free in our choices? Do we find ourselves saying: Let us give it all up. It's useless. We can't do it. It doesn't make sense. We feel foolish. Peter, who will later deny Jesus when he has a choice, at this time speaks on behalf of all the apostles when he says that we all need to have a deeper faith. The apostles will always be able to share Jesus' question with us—"Do you want to leave me too?"—and what effect it had on them in their decision. Sometimes it seems that the choice we

52

have to make is between a closer following of Jesus and no following at all.

The context of our prayer today is the Ignatian Three Types of Persons exercise. It gives us the background to look at what seems to get in the way of our belonging to Jesus. Here is where we find sin lurking in our lives of dedication. It is where Satan tempts. It is the area of disorder in our loves, our affect, and how it calls into question our commitment to Jesus. Our Ignatian sin centers around our avoiding the decisions for our closer following of Jesus. We face many times such decisions, in small and in large ways, in our faith life. Followers of Jesus like the Apostles, from their experience, can help us look at some of these areas in our life.

I suggest for your prayer contemplations three scripture passages. The first contemplation is Matthew 16: 13-23, dealing with Peter's recognition of Jesus. The second prayer period may look to Luke 9: 51-56, where James and John are sure that they know how to handle those who do not follow Jesus—in their way. The third prayer period might take up John 6: 52-69, where Jesus makes hard requests of his followers. The grace we seek this day is the grace to ask forgiveness for our reluctance in drawing closer to Jesus and the grace to make the choices that lead to a closer following of Jesus.

53

Third Day

The Ignatian Three Classes: Choosing to Respond

Review Outline

- the Three Classes of Men is an Ignatian case study about making decisions
- the consistency of our following Jesus is found in our decision-making
- belonging to Jesus remains a day-to-day choice in both our small and large decisions
- our Ignatian sin may be in the ways that we put off the choice to follow Christ more closely

Prayer Points

1) Matthew 16:13-23
2) Luke 9:51-56
3) John 6:52-69

54

Prayer

Jesus, you remain always faithful to us.

We confess that we fail to be so true

in our following of you.

We find ourselves led by what we like.

We know our attachments make us less free.

Strengthen us, we pray, in our every decision

to choose to follow you ever more closely.

Jesus, be our power and our light.

Amen.

Prayer for the Fourth Day

Jesus, you instruct us to learn of you
for you are meek and humble of heart.
We find that hard to hear.
We want to be your apostles,
sent forth to preach fearlessly
and to fight what's evil boldly.
We want to storm the battlements of injustice.
We want to forge our way to new frontiers.
Help us to understand your way of proceeding.
Make us strong with your strength in our mission.
Jesus, be our shepherd and leader.
Amen.

Jesus' Program Imaged In The Two Standards

We have all heard the phrase "Get with the program." As an integral part of our exploring what it means to belong to Jesus, it is necessary for us to look at the program Jesus proposes to his followers. If we turn to the Gospels, some may say that the best summary of Jesus' program is found in the Sermon on the Mount in St. Matthew. Others might want to point to some combination of parables as better imaging the program of Jesus when he talks about the Kingdom.

How might we want to speak about a *program* in relation to what Jesus is preaching about? From the synoptic Gospels, it is evident that Jesus does not preach about himself, but preaches about the Kingdom. The Kingdom is usually identified as "the Kingdom of heaven" or "the Kingdom of God." Matthew is the Gospel writer who has Jesus refer to the Kingdom of heaven—not "heaven" as a place, but rather heaven being an indirect way of referring to God, a title that the Jewish people did not usually

57

articulate. Matthew, being a good Jew and writing for a predominantly Jewish (Christian) community, carefully uses the indirect reference to God by his expression, the Kingdom of heaven, as a way of Jesus' preaching. Jesus usually does not identify himself as the One who is in charge of or is the owner of the kingdom. An exception is found in St. John's Gospel during the interrogation of Jesus by Pilate. Jesus seems to acknowledge the title *king* when Pilate asks the direct question, "Are you a king?" But in John's Gospel, the image of the kingdom is not how Jesus preaches. Whose kingdom is it? Perhaps we are more caught up in the same kind of problem that we touched on when we were describing the "initiative" of the call, whether the initiative is taken by Jesus or by God the Father. For Jesus, it is the kingdom of his Father; for us who listen to Jesus, we tend to identify the kingdom with the One who preaches about it—Jesus.

With our Ignatian formation through the Spiritual Exercises, we identify with Jesus as king in the prayer exercise the Call of the King. When we want to speak of Jesus' program, we would identify it, not so much with the word *kingdom*, but with the Ignatian exercise of the Two Standards. For Ignatius, there was a clarity about what it means to belong to Jesus, the program that we were following in our following of Jesus. For Ignatius, Jesus makes it clear that we understand our belonging to him in terms of poverty, powerlessness, and humility. First, Jesus speaks out consistently that everything he has is gift from God his Father. In fact, in John's Gospel, Jesus goes so far as to say that he has no words, no message, except what the Father would have him say. And if you look at his deeds, they are only what God would have him do. His works, as Jesus says, are the work of God. He literally has nothing of himself; he is truly poor because everything that he is and has is gift.

Now consider if you were starting a new project and trying to enlist people to participate. Imagine trying to start a program with people who have nothing. Surely a program that starts out with people priding themselves on having nothing is a losing program. *That* is where Jesus begins and where he asks us, his followers, to come on board, if we want to be with him.

But, worse yet, how can you have a program that isn't based on some kind of power and influence? What if you preach a program that is powerless because the people living the program claim for themselves no power? Everyone knows from experience that poor people lack power. They are subject to people who have money, those who have influence, and those who exercise power. Jesus in his birth was homeless, in his infancy was a refugee, in his public life was a begging preacher, and on the cross was a humiliated failure who could not save himself. Jesus lived the program that he preached. He did not claim power. He invites his followers to do the same.

And so Jesus bluntly tells us that to be a part of his program we must "learn" of him for he is meek and humble of heart. Jesus entered into the rock-bottom truth of his life. He knew who he was. He was Son of God. No mere human could give that identity to him; no human could take it away from him. It is the God-given truth of his existence. Humility, coming from the Latin word *humus* meaning *ground* or *ground-level*: that's where Jesus stands—at the ground level. That is where Jesus meets us, when we have our feet on the ground. Humility—to be humble—was an essential part of Jesus' life and played an essential part in his program.

As Ignatius imaged it, then, the outline of Jesus' program was quite simple and stark. Jesus' program is not a list of do's and don'ts. It is a program that starts with ourselves—who we really are, at our ground level—and our

59

values. If we accepted the outline of the program, then we could watch and listen to Jesus fill in many details of the program and not find ourselves confused or in denial by what seems in Jesus' message contradictory of common sense. What seems at first to make no human sense makes eminent sense, maybe we should say "divine" sense, when we see how consistently human beings pursue false ideals of success and happiness. Ignatius demonstrates the "making sense" of Jesus' position by contrasting it with the position of that dark angel of light, Lucifer, who stands for all the apparent, alluring fulfillments of human desires—riches, honor, and pride—that take little account of God. Jesus' program, by contrast, is totally focused on "belonging" to God. If we follow Jesus' program, we find ourselves "belonging" to Jesus and so "belonging" to God. That is how in the exercise of the Two Standards Ignatius introduces us into the program of Jesus.

Turning to the Gospels, we are struck by how many images and parables Jesus uses in talking about the Kingdom. For example, the whole of chapter 13 of St. Matthew's Gospel is a collection of the reign of God images. Each of the images used by Jesus tells us in a poetic way something of the way of imaging this kingdom and program which Jesus is proposing for us his followers. To speak of a kingdom to the Jews of Jesus' day would ordinarily have an earthly meaning—some kind of restoration of the Davidic kingdom that God had promised would last forever. After the miracle of the multiplication of the loaves, the crowds wanted to make Jesus king. It seems frequently the apostles would ask him if he was going to set up his kingdom. And, of course, John and James, want to sit at his right and at his left when he comes into his kingdom. Jesus says that they do not know what they are asking because in eventual reality, as Jesus reigns from the cross, there are two criminals also on

60

crosses, on his right and on his left. So Jesus needs to break through the locked-in notions of kingdom present in people in order to let God's notion of kingdom break through. He will use surprising images and parables to try to open up our imaginations, that we might be as creative as God is creative.

Now let us look at the text of Matthew 13. The first image for Jesus' understanding of kingdom is the sower and the seed and the different places where the seed falls. The second image is the field where good seed was sown and then weeds grow too and are left there until harvest time. The third image is the mustard seed and the large bush that is its growth. The fourth image is the yeast that a woman kneads into flour, causing the whole mass to rise. The fifth image is the buried treasure found in a field for which everything is given up in order to purchase that field. The sixth image is the one really valuable pearl for which all the other ones are sold. The final image is the dragnet thrown into the lake which collects all kinds of things—the things of value are kept and the useless are thrown away.

In teaching about the reign of God, Jesus knows that he is also teaching about himself. There is a certain truth when we identify the reign of God and Jesus. Jesus is the definitive breaking in of the reign of God into our human world. The images often describe this kind of presence or breaking in that changes everything. In our effort to belong to Jesus, we too are identified with this breaking in of the reign of God. As we remember, Jesus also says, "The kingdom of God is within you." In these images of the kingdom of God from Matthew's Gospel, we see not only Jesus and his way of acting but we also see ourselves imaged.

The Kingdom of God is not something we build, despite our popular hymn "Let us build the Kingdom of

61

God." The Kingdom of God is not something we can make happen. As Jesus well knew, the Kingdom is God's work. What we do is more passively described: we surrender, we uncover, we let it shine out. And so the images that Jesus uses are about growth in nature—the seed, the wheat, the mustard tree. Growth happens. We can nurture it, we can rejoice in it, and we can stifle it. The Kingdom is like this growth in nature. Jesus is like this growth for us. We, the followers of Jesus, are like this growth for others and for our world. Jesus is the pearl uncovered in the field of the world; we too can be such a pearl. So, too, the Kingdom is like a field of wheat, which we are, but we also include weeds in our field. We can be identified with that field of wheat and the weeds might be identified often with our misguided efforts to "build" the Kingdom. So too the dragnet that collects all kinds of things; this is a shining out of the Kingdom. It is also a picture of us with valuable things, and with the useless things that again are our misguided efforts to make the Kingdom happen.

We are the seed, we are the harvest field, we are the treasure, we are the pearl, we are the dragnet. We can only yield the good—really be identified with the reign of God—if we belong to Jesus, if we are part of his program. When we are part of the program, these images describe our part in making the Kingdom present. We uncover it, we let it shine out, and we point to its presence. The demands of being part of the kingdom are great, but the results are way beyond our imagining. Does Ignatius's way of introducing Jesus and his program in the Two Standards help us to enter into these images of the kingdom?

Another way for us to understand our being part of Jesus' program is to examine our actions. I suggest that we look at the Sermon on the Plain in St. Luke's Gospel to hear from Jesus how we are to act if we are a part

62

of his program. We find the passage in Luke 6: 17-49. Just as Jesus is identified with the Kingdom of God, so I believe that we must read this sermon on the plain in Luke's Gospel as Jesus speaking out of his experience. He is not laying down rules of conduct for others. He is not speaking platitudes. He is telling us that this is the way he lives. If we want to follow him, if we intend to belong to him, this is what he is asking us to do.

Whereas Matthew's portrayal of the Sermon on the Mount has Jesus as the new Moses on a different Mount Sinai setting forth the behavior of those who belong to this new covenant, Luke pictures Jesus standing on the plain (standing being a position of authority) and the plain representing the broad scope of speaking out to a whole world. In his recent book *Jesus of Nazareth*, Benedict, our pope, reflects that the Beatitudes which begin the Sermon are "words of promise. He goes on to say, "At the same time, though, they are criteria for the discernment of spirits and so they prove to be directions for finding the right path (p 71)." It is true that Jesus is looking out at his disciples, and he sees them as poor, meek, weeping, hungry people. Benedict reflects that "These statements are meant to list practical, but also theological, attributes of the disciples of Jesus—of those who have set out to follow Jesus" (p 71) and to identify themselves as belonging to him.

The Beatitudes are paradoxes—just as Ignatius saw it, the standards of the world are turned upside down in terms of God's values, so different from the world. What Jesus declares *blessed*, we must understand with the same reverence that Elizabeth declares Mary "blessed among women." Our sometimes modern translation of the Beatitudes using the word *happy* does not capture what is meant. *Blessed* is to be graced by God, to be highly favored in the divine sight. Jesus first knows himself as *blessed*, and he speaks from his experience. Jesus is speaking out a transformation of values as lived in the Kingdom of God. When we begin to see and live out of this new perspective, when we live as companions of Jesus in his program, then we are living by a new standard. As Jesus promises and knows from his experience, there is already a joy in the freedom in which we will be living with Jesus.

Because the Beatitudes represent where Jesus lives, by our living of these Beatitudes we apply the paradigm of his life to our own lives. As Benedict says, "the Beatitudes display the mystery of Christ himself, and they call us into communion with him" (p 74). When Benedict identifies the Beatitudes as a road map for the Church, we can easily say that the Beatitudes are a roadmap for us for what we should be as the ones recognized as his Ignatian companions. As Jesus closes this discourse, he stresses that unless we build on a rock foundation, our house will collapse. Jesus, above all, is the rock foundation of the kingdom upon which we build, and he has spelled out how we in our own mysterious way help to bring about God's kingdom, acting the way Jesus acts.

As we enter into our prayer periods today, I suggest that we might return to the Ignatian exercise of the Two Standards *Sp Ex* [136]-[147]. We note that we pray for the gift of understanding, for Christ gives us a program of values that boggle our minds. Then we might move in our second prayer period to a consideration of the images of the kingdom that we find in Matthew 13: 1-53. Remember that Jesus is pointing to how the Kingdom is coming about. Think sometimes of how the image is about Jesus and how Jesus is breaking into our lives. Think also of the image as ourselves and how we or what we do is a breaking in of the Kingdom into our world. I believe that you will find a *lectio divina* approach helpful as your way of entering into prayer on this passage from

Matthew. As you know, *lectio divina* is a careful, slow reading of the text, with time for pauses, sometimes dwelling on certain words or phrases, at other times making application to self. The reading may be done once or may be repeated more than once.

For your third period of prayer, I propose the Sermon on the plain passage from St. Luke's Gospel, ch 6, vv 17-49. The passage itself would seem to call upon us in our meditative abilities. We need to drink them in, try to understand the words, and then stir up our own desires to live in such a way. But we could also use the Ignatian contemplative approach. We need to see Jesus speaking, to hear his voice as he invites us to live as he lives, to watch his eyes as he looks at his disciples. We need to look at his listeners, to watch their response, to feel how their hearts burn within them. We need to make our own response.

The grace we seek is to know Jesus more intimately that we might follow him more closely, and so truly belong to him.

65

The Fourth Day

Jesus' Program Imaged in the Two Standards

Review Outline

- Jesus preaches the Kingdom as his program, but what is the Kingdom?
- Ignatius summarizes the program of Jesus in his exercise the Two Standards
- We need to follow the many images of the Kingdom to understand Jesus and his efforts and ourselves and our efforts
- We listen to Jesus' sermon on the plain to know how to act with his values

Prayer Points

1) The Two Standards [136]-[147]
2) Matthew 13:1-53
3) Luke 6:17-49

66

Prayer

Jesus, you instruct us to learn of you

for you are meek and humble of heart.

We find that hard to hear.

We want to be your apostles,

sent forth to preach fearlessly

and to fight what's evil boldly.

We want to storm the battlements of injustice.

We want to forge our way to new frontiers.

Help us to understand your way of proceeding.

Make us strong with your strength in our mission.

Jesus, be our shepherd and leader.

Amen.

Prayer for the Fifth Day

Jesus, we remember well your words at La Storta,
"We want you to serve Us."
But you, Lord, risen as you are,
are carrying a cross.
Well we know that in following you
we serve by carrying our crosses.
You know how weak and inconstant
we, your followers, can be in facing the cross.
By your compassionate love for us,
make us bold in living our ordinary lives of service.
Jesus, be for us our redeemer and savior.
Amen.

The La Storta Vision
As the Icon of Our Belonging

Father Pedro Arrupe was greatly devoted to the La Storta vision in Ignatius's life. As part of his devotion, he made sure that the little chapel at La Storta was restored in the latter years of his being Jesuit superior general. We delegates at General Congregation 33 had a special prayer service there in the newly renovated chapel with Father Arrupe at the time of his resignation as general. As Father Arrupe said, "I am immensely consoled at finding myself in this hallowed place to give thanks to God on arriving at journey's end." He then repeated what he had said in his resignation speech, "And now more than ever I find myself in the hands of this God who has taken hold of me."

At the time, I myself had not been captured by the special vision that Ignatius had at this little chapel before he and his companions entered Rome to minister and eventually to be approved as the Society of Jesus. For me, it was a late discovery appreciating how rich and significant this vision was for Ignatius and is for us in the Society and for all those who find life in Ignatian spirituality. Ignatius makes what seems like a passing reference to the vision in his *Autobiography* [96]. He writes: "One day, a few miles before reaching Rome, he was at prayer in a church and experienced such a change in his soul and saw so clearly that God the Father placed him with Christ his Son that he would not dare doubt it—that God the Father had placed him with his Son." Ignatius recalls this vision again in his *Spiritual Diary* when he identifies

69

the moment when the Father placed him with his Son bearing the cross. Among his early companions, Laínez and Nadal both noted the importance of this vision for Ignatius and for the Society. Some years ago the recently resigned superior general Father Kolvenbach in a homily at the Church of St. Ignatius in Rome proclaimed, "The vision of La Storta has not been given to us so that we might stop to gaze at it. No, it is the light in which the Jesuit [and, I would add, anyone finding life in Ignatian spirituality] regards the whole world."

The details of this vision are not consistently described since the words seem to be an oral tradition shared by Ignatius with various members of the early companions. We do know that Ignatius and his companions were coming to Rome to offer themselves to the service of the pope. Their first intention as a group apostolate—following what they thought was Christ's lead in spending their lives in the Holy Land—had been defeated by circumstances of weather and hostile forces. It is my surmise that, although they had all agreed to a Plan B, offering themselves to the service of the pope, the great discerner Ignatius felt a little uneasy. Was he losing his closeness to Christ? Was he no longer on the same wave length in his discerning? Typical of Ignatius, he went to the most powerful intercessor—Mary, our Lady—and on his way to Rome began praying his mantra-prayer, asking her to place him with her Son. The answer to his prayer is the vision at La Storta. The vision consistently identifies two persons appearing to Ignatius, God the Father and Jesus carrying his cross. Ignatius seems to hear the words "I will be propitious (favorable) to you at Rome." Clearly in the vision the Father turns to Jesus and says, "I want you to take this man to serve us." And Jesus—the Risen Jesus, but carrying his cross—says to Ignatius, "We want you to serve us." Because the *you* was expressed in plural form,

Ignatius understood not only he, but all the companions of Jesus, were included in the desire to serve God. Today, especially, we hear the word *you* as including all of us living an Ignatian spirituality.

For Ignatius, Mary had come to his aid, and he now had confirmation that Jesus truly did identify him as belonging to him. In another way, Ignatius understood the experience of this vision as the confirmation of his own colloquy at the end of the Two Standards exercise—a prayer he had first made twenty-five years earlier. He had been confirmed in being received under the standard of Christ. But more—Ignatius could not doubt it for himself, but he also could not doubt it for the Company of Jesus. We do not doubt it for all of us living an Ignatian spirituality.

We have two conflicting images here with which to work: Christ who is risen and Christ carrying the cross. This is the challenge that Ignatius saw would remain with the Society of Jesus and with all who follow an Ignatian spirituality. We serve the Risen Christ. The victory is won. Death has been defeated, and all the powers that seem to be death-dealing have been overcome. We have been called by the Risen Christ, and we find ourselves serving under the standard of the Risen Christ. The world that we serve is the reconciled world—reconciled in Christ—a world redeemed and a world upon which the Kingdom is breaking in. Ignatian spirituality is known as a world-affirming spirituality. We do not condemn the world and its cultures. We try to find God's goodness in it. But—an important *but*—the Risen Christ continues to carry his cross in all aspects of *our* life—in our personal life, in our family and community life, and especially in our Ignatian mission. If the cross is not a part of our life, we might want to ask whether we have lost our contact with Christ.

Yet at the same time it remains a deep part of Ignatian and Jesuit spirituality that we do not *focus* our spirituality

71

on the passion and suffering of Jesus, as certain spiritualities such as Passionist do. We expect to seek and find God in all things, and we expect to live in a gratitude of gifts given. We do not develop a prayer theory of darkness of soul or feeling abandoned by God, as certain spiritualities such as Carmelite do. I tend to disagree strongly with those writers who try to blend Ignatian prayer and Carmelite prayer, especially represented in the writings of John of the Cross. Their attempt to integrate these different spiritualities shows that they neither understand Carmelite prayer nor do they understand Ignatian prayer. Yes, Ignatius acknowledges desolation as part of our spiritual life, but it is something against which we fight and always seek God's help and favor. Ignatius expects that for a Jesuit to live this Jesuit way of life well God wants for him to be ordinarily in consolation. So, too, is the flow of a spiritual life lived in an Ignatian spirituality. As Ignatius identified himself in his *Autobiography* as a man of devotion, so we are meant to be people of devotion, that is, as Ignatius describes *devotion* as an ease in finding God. If we have an ease in finding God, it means that we are a people living in consolation. We are living as Ignatian spirituality would have us live—finding God in all things.

The vision at La Storta confirmed for Ignatius and for us that the cross will necessarily be an integral part of our following Jesus, the Risen Christ. Strange as it may be to say it, the cross for us will come to us in the *ordinary* course of our daily living—in our ordinary ways of praying, in our ordinary ways of living family life, in our ordinary ways of living out our Ignatian mission. Yes, we will always have our Ignatian exceptions to the ordinary—our extraordinary martyrs who suffer mightily, our certain chosen people of prayer who find God in darkness. More overwhelming in numbers, we have men like Francis Xavier and Peter Canisius and John Francis Regis

72

and Karl Rahner and Teilhard de Chardin and Pedro Arrupe—all of whom found the Risen Christ carrying his cross in their ordinary lives. For us all, to follow the Risen Christ carrying his cross is our Ignatian vocation.

The problem for us is to rise to the occasion of living the ordinary. We look to God's grace when the special moments of God's trials come in our lives. At those traumatic times, we know that we do not have the power within us, and so we readily acknowledge our dependence on God. But when we deal with the *ordinary*, we too readily look to our own insight and our own strength. This is the temptation that comes to us as we face "carrying the cross" in our ordinary lives. We often find ourselves failing to carry the cross. We take measures to avoid it. We reject it. We run from it by our deliberate choices of escape. And yet it is in carrying the everyday crosses of life that we discover the ordinary way in which we belong to Christ.

Perhaps that is why Ignatius was insistent in his directions for each of the contemplative prayer periods in the Third Week that we understood that we were still following Christ. Following Jesus did not end with the Second Week of the Exercises. In the Third Week, we were not just *watching* Jesus in his passion journey, but we were, by God's grace, allowing Jesus to let us accompany him. We want to follow where Jesus leads. For each of the prayer periods in Jesus' passion, Ignatius stresses our journeying with Jesus by his choice of the directional words *from* and *to*. In each prayer period he emphasizes the setting, for example, *from* the garden *to* the house of Annas, and *from* the house of Caiphas *to* Pilate, even *from* the descent from the cross *to* the tomb. We are always there, following Jesus from one place to another throughout his passion and death. We are not observing Jesus; we are following him.

The challenge of following Jesus into the Third Week contemplations of the Exercises is a special challenge for

73

us because it marks the way that we understand the ordinariness of our "carrying the cross" as a way of being brought closer to the Risen Christ. The dailyness of our cross journey is not dramatic and eye-catching, for our spirituality is focused, not on a beaten, bloodied Christ, but on the Risen Christ to whom we belong. That the cross will be an essential part of our daily following of Jesus is a given in Ignatian spirituality and confirmed in the vision of La Storta.

For our prayer, I recommend that we ponder scripture passages that reflect people who with all good will keep asking Jesus about the Kingdom when he speaks of suffering and death. Perhaps our contemplative prayer with them can help us to embody the carrying of the cross in our own daily following of Christ ever more closely.

I propose the scripture passage from Mark 10:35-45 which is sometimes titled the ambition of James and John. You remember how James and John take the initiative and approach Jesus to ask for seats at his right and left hand when he comes into his kingdom. James and John are correct in seeing a right and left hand as Jesus comes into his kingdom, but it just so happens that there are crosses to the left and to the right of Jesus and not thrones. Jesus bluntly tells them that they do not know what they are asking. And then Jesus asks directly: "Can you drink the cup I shall drink of or be baptized in the same bath of pain as I?" Their self-reliance betrays these good-hearted men. "We can," they say boldly. Now all Jesus' apostles want a piece of the action and show their indignation at any one of them getting ahead. So Jesus has to say to them all what the case will be like for all his followers. He points out that he has come to serve. He does not so much talk of pain and suffering, but rather of the *cost* of serving, even to the giving away of one's life. It is the action of service following from love. From the Exercises, we know it as *en todo amar y servir*, "in all things to love and to serve." We seek a more intimate following of Jesus through our loving service. Do we experience the cross in our everyday attempt to serve?

The second passage I suggest is from Luke 22:54-62, the passage of Peter's denial. We all remember how Peter claimed that he was ready to follow Jesus all the way "at his side to face imprisonment and death." His threefold denial is all the sadder because it takes Peter from saying that "no, he was not in the garden with Jesus," to then responding that "no, he was not one of his followers," to finally swearing that "no, he did not even know the man." It was then that Jesus turned around and looked at Peter, and Peter remembered the word the Lord had spoken. He went out and wept bitterly. From Peter, we learn that we, too, often depend upon our own resources when we are intent upon following Jesus. And our ways of denying our following of Jesus happen in increments, like Peter's being questioned more than once. Maybe it's the values that we eventually start living that are no longer so closely identified with Jesus' values. Perhaps it is our language or our ways of dealing with others that are not the ways that Jesus speaks or deals with others in carrying his cross. Our daily following of Jesus more closely takes in necessarily our carrying of the cross with Jesus. Denying our little crosses is our little way of denying that we know Jesus. In our prayer, Peter can sympathize with us about how hard it is.

The third passage I suggest is a brief three lines from Mark 14:50-52. For Mark, these lines sum up the challenge to every follower of Jesus. Can we follow Jesus up to the end? Mark writes, "all deserted him and fled. There was a young man following him who was covered by nothing but a linen cloth. As they seized him, he left the cloth behind and ran off naked." Just as Mark's Gospel began with the call of Jesus to his first followers and they immediately

75

left all—their boats, their families, and friends, so now too as Jesus looks forward to carrying his cross, his followers in the Gospel are dramatically seen as "leaving all" and fleeing naked. Every follower faces the choice in belonging to Jesus: we left all to follow; are we now moving in the direction of leaving all and *not* following?

We are praying for the grace to draw ever more closely to Jesus, knowing our following includes carrying the cross. We want the grace to belong to Jesus, no matter the cost.

The Fifth Day

The La Storta Vision as the Icon of Our Belonging

<u>Review Outline</u>

- the vision at La Storta has special meaning for Jesuits and those finding life in Ignatian spirituality to follow Christ
- Ignatian spirituality does not focus on passion/ death or on darkness in prayer
- the cross in Ignatian spirituality comes in the ordinary following of the Risen Jesus
- Third Week passion contemplations only continue our journey of following Jesus

<u>Prayer Points</u>

76

1) Mark 10:35-45
2) Luke 22:54-62
3) Mark 14:50-52

Prayer

Jesus, we remember well your words at La Storta,

"We want you to serve Us."

But you, Lord, risen as you are,

are carrying a cross.

Well we know that in following you

we serve by carrying our crosses.

You know how weak and inconstant

we, your followers, can be in facing the cross.

By your compassionate love for us,

make us bold in living our ordinary lives of service.

Jesus, be for us our redeemer and savior.

Amen.

Prayer for the Sixth Day

Jesus, you are the Risen One
whom no doors or walls can keep out,
only those whose hearts are hardened.
We sometimes fear to let you surprise us
with your loving presence.
We find it hard to believe
that you pursue us with such love.
We thank you for your resurrection gifts
of forgiveness, of faith, and of love.
Help us ever to follow you more closely.
Jesus, be our peace and our reconciliation.
Amen.

How Do We Belong To the Risen Christ?

Much has been made over the fact that Ignatius begins the Fourth Week of the Spiritual Exercises with Jesus' appearance to Mary—an incident not reported in the Gospels. Many have interpreted it as the personal devotion of Ignatius coming through in this prayer exercise. I would like to interpret it in a little more theological way.

I believe that Ignatius was struck by the consistency in the Gospel resurrection appearances where the risen Jesus is not recognized by his followers. It is not due to the fact that they knew Jesus had died and some of their number had buried him in a nearby tomb. At times, they seem to think of him as a ghost, and he is determined to show them his hand wounds and the wound in his side to prove that he is still the same embodied person. He even takes to asking for something to eat, and seems content with the dried fish that they shared with him. No, there is something more in the fact that they do not recognize him, as the two disciples on the road to Emmaus or Mary Magdalene in the garden, or think that they know who he is but are afraid to ask. What are the Gospel writers trying to tell us about Jesus in his risen life?

It seems to me that the writers are telling us that Jesus is making contact with us, in the fullness of his human-

79

ity, from the other side of the veil. The veil—it may be a funny kind of image, but life-after-death remains mysterious for us. Sometimes we may think of those who have died as "up there" and we are "down here." I prefer the "veil" image—something like a sheer stage curtain that separates us. At times we can be nudged or touched by someone on the other side of the curtain. Sometimes we just feel their presence or support. Jesus is on the other side of that veil or curtain. And he breaks through to us. He is living the resurrected life—the risen life after death—and it sets up a whole new way of relating to us. The newness of the relationship with the Risen Jesus is pictured in the "not recognizing," and "not wanting to ask if it really was he."

For Ignatius who has set up each Week of his Exercises with the grace of a new and deeper relationship with God (with Jesus), the Fourth Week stands apart from the other Three Weeks, just as the resurrection appearances stand apart from the public life and ministry of Jesus. Like the apostles, like Mary Magdalene, we too must let Jesus introduce us to a new and deeper relationship with him through the graces of the Fourth Week. When we are in the total Exercises experience, the wonderful grace of the Second Week of knowing Jesus more intimately that we might love him more and follow him more closely is followed by the still more wonderful grace of being invited by Jesus to follow him compassionately in his journey of handing himself over to belong totally to God and to us in the Third Week. But both of these marvelous graces pale in comparison with the intimacy called for by the Risen Jesus who wants to come into our lives.

80

That is the more theological reason why Ignatius chooses to have us enter into the Fourth Week contemplations through our contemplation of the Risen Jesus appearing to Mary his mother. Mary is the one who has had the most intimate relationship possible to the human Jesus. She, his mother, has carried him in her womb for nine months. She has known the intimacy of carrying that new life within her. She has nursed her newborn Son with the milk of her breasts. She has held him to her heart. She did all the things that loving mothers do. After the Cana incident, which surely is another occasion of seeing a loving intimacy between mother and son, sporadic are the appearances of Mary with Jesus in his public ministry. Her grace of compassionate intimacy with Jesus in his suffering and death could also have been used by Ignatius in introducing us to the Third Week. Mary was the first to know that Third Week grace of compassion, and one visible way of capturing it for all of us is in Michelangelo's *Pietà*. Yet for Mary and for us, relating to Jesus in his passion and death is still relating to the human Jesus. Ignatius probably did not think that he needed to focus on Mary's special help for us to enter into the Third Week.

When Jesus pierces through the veil that separates us in this life from those who live in eternal life with God, even Mary his mother needs to acknowledge a wholly new relationship. How we struggle to describe the newness of the intimacy between Mary and Jesus! That is why we contemplate. All our words fail us, just as words about the Risen Jesus relating to his followers failed the gospel writers. That the Risen Jesus is embodied, that is, risen from the dead in his full humanity, is the foundation of our belief in the life of the resurrection. In our own risen life, we will not be living in some sort of a spiritual world. It is beyond our feeble imaginings, but in the coming of the Kingdom there will be a new heavens and a new earth, as the Book of Revelation tells us. This new heavens and a new earth—in continuity with our present heavens and earth, just as our risen body will be in continuity with the body that is ours now—are all part of the Kingdom to come. But Jesus is the first fruits of this new life. And Jesus, embodied as he is, is not hindered by doors or walls, by distances, or by time. His love is no longer expressed by a hug; his very being interpenetrates our very being. Eucharistic communion is a foretaste, a touching in of this experience with Jesus. In her risen Son, Mary had to experience a loving intimacy that was light years beyond even carrying him in her womb. Only Mary can share with us from her experience that, whatever intimacy we may have felt with Jesus as we pray his life of ministry in the Second and Third Weeks of the Exercises, the intimacy is beyond all telling when the Risen Jesus enters into our life. That is why our contemplation of the Risen Jesus appearing to Mary is key to all our contemplations of the resurrection. She, the most privileged person in knowing intimacy, can guide us through her experience in our own entering into the special intimacy with the Risen Jesus.

While it is true that we are following the Risen Jesus, we must remember that we are always following the One who is carrying the cross. Like the apostles and Mary, we are graced for a *limited time* to be with Jesus as we pray the Fourth Week. We do not *live* in the Fourth Week. In fact, as Ignatius so well knew, we would always need to live among all Four Weeks of the Exercises. We never lose our relationship with God (with Jesus) that flows throughout the dynamic or movement of the Exercises. We are always sinners; we need the grace of the First Week. We will always be disciples of Jesus learning his way; we need the grace of the Second Week. We will always need to accompany Jesus in his cross; we need the grace of the Third Week. We will always be graced to follow the Risen Jesus who has called us and is calling us now; we need the grace of the Fourth Week. But what is so special about our relationship with Jesus in the Fourth Week? The Fourth Week of the Exercises introduces us to those special moments of consolation where God touches us in the depth of our being—what Ignatius particularly identifies as a consolation without cause. That is the kind of consoling effect of the Risen Jesus as he invites us to share his joy of victory. It is the grace we pray for in the Fourth Week. The experience of the Fourth Week allows us to know these special moments of consolation when they appear in our ordinary Ignatian spirituality living.

It is important for us to ask Jesus for the grace to experience the intimacy that he wants to share with us in his risen life. The Ignatian contemplations are one way—a privileged way for us following Ignatian spirituality—to enter into the new intimacy that the Risen Jesus offers us. It is the kind of intimacy to which the devotion to the Sacred Heart points, as St. Margaret Mary Alacoque and St. Claude Colombière experienced. It is a heart intimacy.

We may be talking very "spiritual" and what sounds like "ethereal" language here. Let me bring us back to a practical sharing with us that the Risen Jesus does in three different appearances. Jesus shares with his apostles and with us these special graces of consolation. In the first Easter evening appearance that John records in his Gospel (John 20: 19-23), Jesus appears to his disciples behind their locked doors. Remember that they all had fled from Jesus in his passion and death. Only in John's Gospel do we have one—John—being there with Mary. What is the first thing that the apostles need from Jesus? His forgiveness. That is the first gift that the Risen Jesus wants to share with them. He forgives them their cowardice, their betrayal, their rejection of belonging to him. Not only does he forgive, but offers them his gift of forgiveness to share with others. We need to enter into Ignatian contemplative prayer in this passage. How do we know that we have contact with the Risen Jesus? We can experience it in our ways of accepting forgiveness and

83

in our being able to offer forgiveness. Forgiveness is our first contact point with the Risen Jesus. It is his consolation gift to us.

For our second prayer period, I am proposing the appearance of Jesus on the second Sunday after Easter back in the same locked room, but this time with Thomas present. This passage is from John 20: 24-29. Thomas is the center of the Risen Jesus' second gift, but it is the gift that Jesus claims will be his blessing to all his followers. It is the gift of faith. It is our faith, as it was the apostles' faith, that is the most precious gift of the Risen Lord. As St. Paul says, if we have faith in Jesus, but he has not been raised, we are the most pitiable of people. Faith in the Risen Jesus and faith in our own bodily resurrection are keystones of our Catholic faith. We need to contemplate this appearance of Jesus to Thomas carefully. The Risen Jesus' second gift to us his followers is the most precious gift of faith—a consolation gift we often take too lightly. We need always to pray for the gift of faith.

The third passage that I will suggest is from John 21:15-19. It is the familiar passage of Jesus' questioning of Peter about his love. We could interpret Jesus' first question to Peter in two ways. Jesus asks Peter, "Do you love me more than these?" Is Jesus asking Peter whether he (Peter) loves Jesus more than he loves his fellow apostles? Or is Jesus asking Peter whether Peter loves him (Jesus) more than the other apostles love Jesus? Would Peter jump in his presumption to say that, of course, he loves Jesus more than anyone else? We note, however, that Peter is very careful in his response. He says simply, "Yes, Lord, you know that I love you." He is not putting himself in any comparative mode; he is letting it up to the knowledge of Jesus himself about the quality and depth of his love. Jesus answers, "Feed my lambs." We note that service always follows upon love.

84

A second time Jesus puts the question, saying "Simon, son of John, do you love me?" Again Peter does not look to his own resources, but repeats his response, "Yes, Lord, you know that I love you." As he faces this new relationship with the Risen Jesus, Peter has never felt so totally known. He turns over his whole self, with all his strengths and weaknesses, to how Jesus knows him to be as a lover. Jesus simply says, "Feed my sheep." Again service follows upon a profession of love.

It is when Jesus asks a third time, "Do you love me?" that Peter feels the hurt of the question. Peter makes his profession of his total openness to the intimate knowledge that this Risen Jesus has of him. Peter cries out "Lord, you know everything. You know well that I love you." Jesus not only repeats, "Feed my sheep," but goes on to declare that the surrender of love that Peter professes will be the surrender that he will live into his older years and death. The Jesus quietly calls to Peter, "Follow me."

Over the centuries, there has always been the consistent tradition that the three questions of Jesus are meant to match the three denials of Peter. There is little doubt that Peter would make such a relationship between denials and belongings. In our own Ignatian contemplative prayer, we also are aware that the three questions of Jesus need not be restricted to Peter or to us at any one time of our life. Rather as Jesus would indicate in his final response to Peter, the question that Jesus continues to pose to us is about our love many times over in our lifetime.

Like Peter, we come to know that this kind of love, this kind of belonging, is a particular gift of the risen Jesus to us. It is a gift confirmed in Jesus' sending of the Spirit, but it remains a special gifting from the Risen Jesus, not only that we might love Jesus more intimately, but that we might be identified as people who love. Our love source is no longer confined to the meagerness of our own loving powers but now resides in the intimacy we have with the Risen Christ. The Risen Jesus shares his way of loving with us, his followers—a most special consolation gift.

The grace we seek this day is the grace to experience the new intimacy offered by the Risen Christ and the special sharing in his gifts of forgiveness, faith, and love.

The Sixth Day

How Do We Belong to the Risen Christ?

Retreat Outline

- to know the Risen Christ is to experience a wholly new level of intimacy
- Ignatius suggests that Mary is the key person to help us respond to this new way of knowing Jesus
- this new intimacy with the Risen Jesus does not eliminate our consistent need for the graces of all Four Weeks of the Exercises
- the Risen Jesus shares with us three special gifts of his risen life: forgiveness, faith, and love

Prayer Points

1) John 20:19-23
2) John 20:24-29
3) John 21:15-19

86

Prayer

Jesus, you are the Risen One
whom no doors or walls can keep out,
only those whose hearts are hardened.
We sometimes fear to let you surprise us
with your loving presence.
We find it hard to believe
that you pursue us with such love.
We thank you for your resurrection gifts
of forgiveness, of faith, and of love.
Help us ever to follow you more closely.
Jesus, be our peace and our reconciliation.
Amen.

Prayer for the Seventh Day

Jesus, in your risen life you touch us
in those special moments called consolation.
We thank you for the times you walk with us
and make our hearts burn.
We are grateful when we hear you call us by name.
Keep us free from clinging to your consoling presence
so that we can always meet you in new and deeper ways.
Bring home to our hearts that you are always with us.
Jesus, be our resurrection and our life.
Amen.

Belonging Viewed as Three Kinds of Humility

Some commentators on the Exercises have proposed that the exercise known as the Three Degrees of Humility or the Three Kinds of Humility (*Sp Ex* [165]-[168]) is really at the heart of the election of every Ignatian retreat, even if a specific life-direction is being chosen. There is also a certain tradition that suggests that if in the ordinary course of our *annual* retreat we seem to have no one focus or choice in mind, our real focus or "election" is always in terms of the Three Degrees of Humility.

What I appreciate in these views about the Degrees of Humility is the fact that the focus is centered on a relationship with Jesus. Sometimes we seemingly stress the importance of election or life-decision in an Ignatian retreat in such a way that it obscures the fact that every retreat (and *especially* choice or election retreats) is made in the context of a deepening relationship with Jesus. In every retreat, the discernment of a choice is on the comparative testing of whether such a choice enhances or

89

hinders my growing relationship with Jesus. It is not just a choice of mission for anyone living Ignatian spirituality, but it is a choice whether the mission will make our relationship with Jesus closer.

Where, then, do we find Ignatius putting the greatest stress in this relationship with Jesus? I believe that we find it in the consideration called the Three Degrees of Humility—in the full 30-day Spiritual Exercises, a consideration that Ignatius suggests that we make apart from our ordinary prayer exercises sometime after the Fifth Day in the Second Week. In a Note, Ignatius indicates that we might take our reflections to prayer and, using the triple colloquy, ask that our Lord choose us for the third and greatest degree of humility.

Because the Ignatian title does not make perfectly clear what the consideration is about, some commentators prefer to change the title from using the word *humility* to the word *love*. This would seem to make clear that the exercise is about relationship and not about acquiring some virtue. There are also the differing attempts to say, whether we use either the word *humility* or *love*, that we are speaking more of ways or modes rather than degrees. Although I think that a case can be made for speaking about different ways or manners of exercising humility or of being loving, I am inclined to favor the word *degree* since we can think of colder or warmer levels. Colder and warmer seem to fit with the notion of our relationships. We have warmer relations with some people than with others. We certainly can experience a cool relationship with people who do not respect us or sometimes disagree with us.

Ignatius's use of the word *humility* flows from the image of Jesus given by him in the Two Standards. Jesus identifies himself with humility. It is the essence of his very being. He knows who he is—the Son of God. In the mystery of the Trinitarian life, the Son is the image, the reflection of God the Father from all eternity. And the Spirit is the Person of love that they share. Jesus is grounded in the truth of his being. *That* is his humility.

In the Ignatian approach to our belonging to Jesus, we gain some experience of our closeness by our own living the life of a humble person. Ignatius would have us realize that there is an element of our choice involved. As one half of the parties involved in this friendship, we have a certain freedom in determining how close we want to draw to Jesus, how much we want the very life of Jesus to be reflected in the way that we live. That is the content of the Ignatian reflection called the Three Degrees of Humility.

When Ignatius names three degrees or modes, he is not saying that there are only three. There are as many ways or degrees of loving or being humble as there are human beings. Perhaps we might find it easier to think that the degrees are better pictured as a color spectrum that seems to have an infinite number of shadings of color. What Ignatius points to in specifying three is a certain range of our human behaviors that put us into a measured relationship with Jesus. A rather crude way of describing the various degrees of closeness or intimacy was often used by saying that the first degree imaged by Ignatius was a relationship that was measured by our willingness or not to break off the relationship by mortal sin. In a similar way, the second degree measured our desire for closeness to Jesus in terms of the venial sins that we commit in not fostering the relationship. The third degree brings us into the same openness and availability to God that we find in the third class or type of persons. We are saying to Jesus that we want him to draw us into his friendship so closely that if the externals of his life were to be reflected in our own, it would give us the greatest of joys. We make ourselves totally available to Jesus.

91

We note that in this third degree we acknowledge that Jesus is the other party in this friendship, and Jesus himself has the openness and freedom to draw us closely to himself. We are not demanding to get what we want. I remember someone writing that "we get no deeper into Christ than we allow him to get into us." In a paradoxical way, that probably is still a good restatement of the third degree since it seems that Jesus puts no limits on his openness and desire to draw us deeply into himself.

I think that the problem we might have with the third degree is in our appropriation of what the externals of Jesus' life being reflected in our own might mean. Perhaps we tend to take literally the word *externals* and so if we follow Jesus literally, we want to live like an itinerant preacher, and if a man, having others, especially women just as in the Gospels, take care of all our needs. In a more dramatic way, we might think to look to persecution from people in authority, calling down upon ourselves our own kind of passion and perhaps even death. I don't think that "externals of Christ's life" meant this for Ignatius. Rather Ignatius experienced his way of this third degree in the fact that he was elected the first superior general and had to remain in Rome. Remember he was the one who wanted to spend his life in the Holy Land. He was the one who could imagine the pope sending him off to India; instead he becomes the one who sends his closest companion, Francis Xavier, to a mission that he must have hungered after. He was the man of action, and he spent the later years of his life sitting down at a desk and writing the Constitutions. For Ignatius, this kind of passion of availability to God is the way to his belonging to Jesus in "externals."

92

When God responds to our prayer to be graced with this degree of intimacy imaged in the third degree, it is not for us to picture or to determine what shape the externals of Jesus' life will take in our own living. But that it will include all the elements of the paschal mystery we can be sure. I am reminded of an imaginary dialogue between Jesus and ourselves. Jesus asks: "Why do you not respond when I give you everything that I have?" And our words to Jesus are: "You give me everything that you have, but nothing that I want." We need to remember that the greatest danger to the humble person remains the temptation to pride. We want what we want, and we want it in the way that we imagine it. Even as we try to live humbly, we can become self-focused and self-centered in our spiritual living.

As we enter into the final days of this retreat, I would propose that we enter into prayer that we might be drawn as close in our friendship with Jesus as we can desire. Because we are dealing with the Risen Jesus, I will continue to suggest passages from his risen life. The first passage I offer is the disciples on the road to Emmaus which we find in Luke 24:13-35. You know the incident well, with the two disciples making their way from Jerusalem to Emmaus on that first Easter day and being joined by Jesus, whom of course they do not recognize. How does this passage help us to enter into our consideration about intimacy with Jesus? Remember that these two are followers of Jesus, companions of Jesus. They can relate their esteem and love for him, describing him as "Jesus of Nazareth, a prophet powerful in word and deed in the eyes of God and all the people." They can report about the empty tomb, and women seeing angels saying that Jesus was alive. But then they go back to their self-focus, saying "we were hoping." Jesus chides them for the limits they place on themselves in relating to him, and then kindly gives them a lecture in scripture that would help them read his life. When Jesus seems to indicate that he would continue on his way, they expressed their desires

93

for his staying with them. And then they recognized him in the breaking of the bread. Immediately they could say to each other that he had set their hearts on fire by his presence and his words. "Hearts on fire" was their expression for a new intimacy that the Risen Jesus had given them. It was a consolation moment that sent them back to Jerusalem to share their experience.

The second passage I suggest is from John 20: 11-18. It is Jesus' appearance to Mary Magdalene in the garden. Mary Magdalene had a certain intimacy with Jesus—a closeness identified in the various Gospels by the fact that she is named as a follower, even to the cross. Mary Magdalene, caught up in her own self-focused relationship with Jesus, will not let even the appearance of angels sway her from her sentry effort at the tomb, empty now, but a tomb we now know holds only the past. Even Jesus' questioning, "Woman, why are you weeping?" does not move Mary from her introspective wanting and even holding to a body that is dead. It is when Jesus says her name, "Mary," that she knows the call to a new intimacy. This is where we have the seemingly strange line from Jesus, "Don't cling to me." I suspect that Jesus was just confirming for Mary Magdalene that she was clinging to a past Jesus, a past relationship, and now they were entering into a wholly new intimacy. And wonderful as this moment of a new-felt closeness is, Jesus missions Mary to share the experience with his brothers, the rest of the followers. We might ask ourselves in prayer whether we cling to old relationships and whether we listen to Jesus calling us by name today.

The third passage I propose is Matthew 28: 16-20. This passage deals with Jesus sending forth the apostles in his last appearance to them before he ascends into heaven. For Matthew, Jesus has summoned the apostles back to Galilee, where his public ministry and their calling had first begun. As Matthew records, "at the sight of him, those who had entertained doubts fell down in homage." Once again, remember that we are talking about Jesus' followers, his companions. What are their doubts about? Is it their relationship with Jesus? Is it over? Can it grow? And does "falling down in homage" mean that they are giving themselves over to Jesus in a new intimacy to which he is inviting them? He gives them a mission to the whole world, making "disciples of all the nations." And then comes that most consoling line in all the Gospels, "And know that I am with you always, until the end of the world." Just as Matthew began his Gospel identifying the newborn one of Mary as Emmanuel, God-is-with-us, now Jesus himself confirms that he is the One who is always with us. This is the intimacy promised by the Risen Jesus. In our prayer we might ask ourselves whether we do have doubts about ever being close to Christ or growing in our intimacy. We might want to savor Jesus saying to us "Know that I am with you always."

The grace that we are praying for is that we might choose to be drawn into the deepest friendship that allows Jesus' life to be mirrored in our own.

95

The Seventh Day

Belonging Viewed as Three Kinds of Humility

Retreat Outline

- the Three Degrees of Humility deal with our closeness to Jesus
- Ignatius points the way for us to pray for a most special intimacy
- our confusion about closeness may come in our imagining it by external conformity

Prayer Points

1) Luke 24:13-35
2) John 20:11-18
3) Matthew 28:16-20

96

Prayer

Jesus, in your risen life you touch us
in those special moments called consolation.
We thank you for the times you walk with us
and make our hearts burn.
We are grateful when we hear you call us by name.
Keep us free from clinging to your consoling presence
so that we can always meet you in new and deeper ways.
Bring home to our hearts that you are always with us.
Jesus, be our resurrection and our life.
Amen.

Prayer for the Eighth Day and Final Reflection

Jesus, we thank you for the special time
of being close to you in these days of prayer.
Send us forth with new eyes
to see a world bathed in your redeeming love.
Give us the courage to live our faith,
that in your death and resurrection
all worldly forces have been defeated.
Strengthen us in our mission of reconciling
whatever seems to cause division
in ourselves, in our families, in our mission, in our church.
Jesus, make us holy and keep us full of hope.
Amen.

Thanks-Living in Paul's Letter To the Colossians

As our final reflection time within the retreat, I am proposing that we use a *lectio divina* style of praying as we consider St. Paul's Letter to the Colossians. I believe that it sums up well the theme of our retreat, "To whom do we belong?" Paul's letter also sends us forth with inspired apostolic zeal. I have been stimulated in the reflections that I want to share with you through the work of the contemporary scripture scholar, N.T. Wright, who also serves as the Anglican Bishop of Durham diocese in England. In fact, the only original perspective that I can claim in this presentation is my relating what we find in Paul's letter to what seems to get reflected in our own Ignatian spirituality. So know that I am repeating the insights and expressions of N.T. Wright in this presentation because he truly inspired me to read Paul in relation to Ignatian spirituality in a wholly new way.

Just as we know that gratitude is the pervasive attitude in our living an Ignatian spirituality, so we find Paul's letter to the Colossians speaking out that thankfulness marks the Christian relationship with God. For Paul and for Ignatius, God is the Giver of gifts—gifts so many and so overwhelming that our one response is always a "thank you." We experience daily this orientation of always saying "thank you" as we enter into the first point of our

99

Ignatian examen of consciousness. So the primary relationship that I want to make between Paul's letter and our Ignatian spirituality is the grounding in a spirit of gratitude.

Perhaps it would be helpful for us to have a little background on this letter. Colossae was a small town in present-day Turkey, inland from Ephesus and about midway down in the country. Paul never visited there and so did not begin the church there. The town itself was destroyed by an earthquake, somewhere around AD 64 and was never rebuilt. The ruins of the town today are minimal. The early church there was vibrant enough that Paul has heard of its fervor as well as rumors of some possible areas of turmoil that prompt him to write his letter. The letter is brief; it has been divided traditionally into four chapters.

Paul begins his letter by thanking God for the church there in Colossae. And he urges the Colossians themselves to be thankful to God for the faith they share as a community. The central section of the letter, which begins in chapter 2, stresses again that we must live with an explicit thankfulness. As Paul begins to sum up in chapter 3, he again emphasizes gratitude. Finally in chapter 4 Paul says that we must always pray in a spirit of thanksgiving.

Why is Paul encouraging these Colossians to such a spirit of gratitude? Paul identifies God as gifting them with their faith. God has rescued them from the power of darkness and has brought them into the kingdom of his beloved Son in whom we have redemption and the forgiveness of sin. Why are we grateful? This is the critical and vital theme of Paul's letter: it is the victory of Christ over the powers. We might ask what is Paul talking about when he speaks of these "powers"? This may have been one of the potential turmoil points in this fledgling church.

For ancient peoples this world was full of hostile or potentially hostile forces. It was common to identify these forces as gods. If one were going on a sea voyage, it certainly would be good to propitiate the sea god, sometimes named Neptune. If one were fighting a war, one needed Mars on one's side. (We know from the Old Testament how the battles fought were often seen in terms of one side's gods against the Israelite God. We have read how much the Israelites thought just like their enemies. The people could not understand a defeat if they had this one all-powerful God on their side. Did it mean that the other side's gods were stronger?) If one were in love, one would need the help of Aphrodite. People went about their daily lives in a climate of fear and uncertainty because they were at the mercy of all these various gods and their power.

We may tend to laugh at this kind of behavior in our present day. But consider how we speak of our lives today. With all the disarray of our economic problems what do we say caused it? We say, "It is economic forces." *Forces?* They must be very powerful because they are affecting the whole world. The most powerful people in the world cannot figure it out. All we can do is "try things," we say. Millions of people are out of work. Thousands of businesses are in bankruptcy. We say, "It is economic forces."

Why is peace so hard to come by? We talk about political powers. We speak of tribal allegiances, of ethnic histories. Despite the existence of the United Nations organization, why are we always facing conflicts among the world's peoples? If we have the ability to grow enough food to feed the world's population, why do so many continue to starve? We say that there are forces which stop us from accomplishing it.

We can't see or touch these forces. Sometimes we try to identify the "force" with a person—a political leader, a rebel general—but take away the person, and the force of hatred, division, whatever, remains. Our words today—forces, powers, climate—point to something bigger than the sum total of the human beings involved. We have a set of situations that no one wants, but at the same time no one can do anything about it. The significant difference between ancient peoples and ourselves appears to be that they recognized the situation and gave the forces personal names while we hide behind the gray obscurity of vague words.

It would seem that the people at Colossae were still being tempted by old ways of thinking about these powers. Paul has three things to say to them, in the light of the faith in Jesus that God has given to them. As his first point, in drawing upon what seems to be one of the early Christian hymns, Paul says that all things were created in Christ. And these "things" include what is visible and invisible, whether thrones or dominations, principalities or powers. Everything was created through, in, and for him. Moreover it is only in Christ that everything continues in being. For Paul, this is his Principle and Foundation statement.

If everything, including these powers and forces, is made in Christ, what went wrong? As Paul reflects, human beings gave up their responsibility for God's world and handed their power over to the powers. For example, when human beings refuse to use God's gift of money responsibly, they give over power to Mammon. When human beings refuse to use God's gift of sexuality responsibly, the power of Aphrodite takes over. Ignatius in his Principle and Foundation puts it positively when he says that life is made up of our responsible choices among all of God's gifts as we try to serve God.

In his second point, Paul makes clear to the Colossians that, since they are in Christ, they do not need to submit to any powers. Why was Jesus crucified? He taught a way of being human which challenged the powers at every point. Powers said that you should live for money. Jesus said you cannot serve both God and Mammon. Powers said that Israel's liberation would come through the sword. Jesus said that those who take up the sword would perish by the sword. Powers said that Caesar was Lord of the world. Jesus proclaimed the Kingdom of God.

When we ask the question "why was Jesus crucified?" we are always left with a certain mystery. And who was it that crucified Jesus? Whom can we blame it on? We know the problems that those kinds of questions have caused down to our own day. We might better say powers did him in. On the cross Jesus took on all the principalities and powers. Look at Jesus crucified, and see that powers killed him. Powers nailed up above his head the charge that he was a rebel, he called himself king. Powers stripped him naked and humiliated him. Powers celebrated their triumph over him all the way to his gasping last breath as he surrenders himself to his Father.

But to the Colossians Paul boldly proclaims that the cross was not a defeat for Christ, but a defeat for the powers. The power of the bleeding love of Jesus is stronger than the power of Caesar, Mars, Aphrodite, and Mammon. In his paradoxical way, Paul reverses all the images about crucifixion. He says that God disarmed the principalities and powers by nailing their claims to the cross. He stripped them naked, and they were the defeated ones left captive by the triumph of Christ. This is the reason for the Colossians' gratitude. The battle against powers has been won. As Paul exults, he points out that you Colossians have a share in this victory in him who is over every principality and power.

And that brings Paul to this third point, which probably surprised the Colossians and still surprises us. Although we speak of the defeat of the powers, we do

103

not mean their annihilation. Rather the powers have been reconciled in Christ. God in the Risen Christ is making a new world. This is the kingdom for which we pray in every Our Father. What do we mean by this reconciliation? To say that we must not worship Aphrodite does not mean that we should become sexless beings. To say that we cannot serve God and Mammon does not mean that we should stop using money. To say that racial prejudice is wrong does not mean that we cannot celebrate our differences. God intends all the powers to serve him and to serve and sustain all of us, his children in Christ.

Paul's way of looking at the world and its powers becomes Ignatius's way of appreciating a world that is enveloped in the redeeming love of the Risen Christ. Ignatius would not have us dividing the world into good and evil parts. Creation is from God, and God sees it as good. Ignatius would not have us try to suppress our desires, our loves, and our attachments or call them bad; he would have us "order" them, and the ordering principle is always our belonging to Christ.

Paul suggests in his third chapter to the Colossians that their lives should be ordered by their new faith in Christ. Paul draws some everyday moral examples. Today we are not comfortable with how Paul expresses in this chapter the relation between husbands and wives and between slaves and their masters. He seems to accept readily the customs and cultures of the world in which he lives. But we need to acknowledge that Paul has laid the foundation that in Christ we are all brothers and sisters to one another and we are free of the powers that enslave the wider world in which we live. Even in the midst of a slave culture and in the midst of sex-inequality Paul was saying that *our* behavior can change, and we can live differently because of our relationship to the Risen Jesus. I believe that we still need to hear Paul's suggesting of a way of living in a pagan world that does not accept our values or our freedom from the powers around us. Like Paul, we too need to live a life of reconciliation within a pagan or secular culture if we are to belong to Christ who is, above all, the reconciler. We do not stand apart from the world and critique it. We must witness and we must try to live as Christ's ambassadors of reconciliation. We do not run from this redeemed world. We do not demand a change in the world's behaviors before we change our own.

We are to live in thanksgiving now, not at some time when everyone thinks alike and has the same values as ourselves. I borrow N.T. Wright's expression; we should witness to "thanks-living." Ignatius would wholeheartedly accept that word. We who live an Ignatian spirituality should practice thanks-living. The practical ways are all present in our day-to-day lives. First, the Eucharist, which means thanksgiving, is our central act of living in thanks because we live the action of belonging to Christ. Second, as often as we pray the Lord's prayer, we express our thankful desire that the Kingdom keeps breaking into our world. Third, every time we come to eat—a daily activity—by our grace we express thanks to God for these specific gifts given to us. And fourth, our daily Ignatian examen always recalls for us that we never come to prayer without first thanking God.

Thanks-living describes our life. Why? Because we belong to Christ, and it is Christ who has set us free in the face of our present-day powers. Let us pray for the grace that thanks-living is our Ignatian way of life. And may we be graced to live as reconcilers because we belong to Christ.

The Eighth Day and Final Reflection

Thanks-Living In Paul's Letter To the Colossians

Retreat Outline

- we can read Paul's Letter to the Colossians as Paul's way of expressing the Principle and Foundation and the Contemplation on the Love of God, the "bookends" of the Spiritual Exercises
- Paul's letter is a letter of gratitude, encouraging thanks as the first and basic response to God
- through Jesus' death and resurrection, the power and forces of the world have been defeated and have been reconciled
- our mission is both to live and to preach this newfound freedom in Christ

Prayer Point

A *lectio divina* prayer of the Letter to the Colossians

106

Prayer

Jesus, we thank you for the special time
of being close to you in these days of prayer.
Send us forth with new eyes
to see a world bathed in your redeeming love.
Give us the courage to live our faith,
that in your death and resurrection
all worldly forces have been defeated.
Strengthen us in our mission of reconciling
whatever seems to cause division
in ourselves, in our families, in our mission, in our church.
Jesus, make us holy and keep us full of hope.
Amen.

Books Referenced in the Retreat

Fleming, David L., SJ *Draw Me into Your Friendship. A Literal Translation and a Contemporary Reading of The Spiritual Exercises.* St. Louis: The Institute of Jesuit Sources, 1996.

Divarkar, Parmananda R., SJ. *A Pilgrim's Testament. The Memoirs of St. Ignatius of Loyola as Transcribed by Luis Gonçalves da Câmara.* St. Louis: The Institute of Jesuit Sources, 1995.

Olin, John C. (ed) and John F. O'Callaghan SJ (trans) *The Autobiography of St. Ignatius Loyola, with Related Documents.* New York: Fordham University Press, 1993. First published 1974 by Harper and Row.

Rahner, Karl, SJ *On the Theology of Death.* New York: Herder and Herder, 1961.

Ratzinger, Joseph (Pope Benedict XVI) *Jesus of Nazareth. From the Baptism in the Jordan to the Transfiguration.* New York: Doubleday, 2007.

Wright, N.T. *Following Jesus. Biblical Reflections on Discipleship.* London: SPCK, 1994.

108

Article

Buckley, Michael J., SJ "The Contemplation to Attain Love," *The Way Supplement*, no 24 (1975), 92-104.

Additional Resources from the Author

Fleming, David L., SJ *Discipleship and Its Foundations. A Jesuit Retreat.* St. Louis: Review for Religious, 2005.

—— *What More Can I Do? An Ignatian Retreat for People Somewhere on the Way.* St. Louis: Review for Religious, 2006.

—— *Lessons from Ignatius Loyola.* St. Louis: Review for Religious, 2005.

—— *Like the Lightning. The Dynamics of the Ignatian Exercises.* St. Louis: The Institute of Jesuit Sources, 2004.

—— *What Is Ignatian Spirituality?* Chicago: Loyola Press, 2008.